SMALL EARTHQUAKE IN WILTSHIRE

*Seventeenth-century conflict
and its resolution*

ERIC L JONES

THE HOBNOB PRESS

First published in the United Kingdom in 2017

by The Hobnob Press,
30c Deverill Road Trading Estate, Sutton Veny, Warminster BA12 7BZ
www.hobnobpress.co.uk

British Library Cataloguing in Publication Data
A catalogue record for this book is available from the British Library

ISBN 978-1-906978-47-1

Typeset in Scala 11/14 pt. Typesetting and origination by John Chandler

Printed by Lightning Source

CONTENTS

PROLOGUE

THIS BOOK OPENS with the Penruddock Rising against Oliver Cromwell in 1655, sometimes called the Salisbury Rebellion and heavily featuring the Wiltshire gentry. The Rising is a point of entry into a period described by leading historians as setting the course of English, even world, history for centuries. The episode is therefore worth rescuing from the shadows of history because of its implications for the remainder of the Interregnum, the subsequent Restoration and later periods, as well as for wider geographical areas.

The rebels captured Salisbury but the Rising ended in humiliating defeat. Theirs was a small earthquake in Wiltshire with, as the spoof headline said, not many dead. The episode is sometimes dismissed as a futile side-show but more often ignored altogether. This is misleading, partly because it led to the imposition of the unloved rule by Puritan Major-Generals, and partly because the tale throws open windows on the realities of the seventeenth and later centuries. The opening chapters introduce two of the cast of villains who figured at the period: Martin Noel, scrivener or financier, and John Wildman, professional conspirator. Noel, in particular, inhabits a black hole in an otherwise much studied era. Said to have been possibly the most influential man of his time, and clearly one of the most influential, he lacks even a main entry in the *Dictionary of National Biography*.

Penruddock's Rising was officered by three principals from the Wiltshire gentry, only one of whom avoided beheading. Investigating the third man's unexpected escape led me to grasp the importance of family and local connections in the period. Marriage alliances among their huge families knitted the gentry together. Many of Penruddock's supporters were his own kinfolk and those who were not were often related to someone in the conspiracy. Personal ties pulled them into the Rising and sometimes pulled them out of the consequences; society's institutions were too ramshackle to be entirely relied on. They gave the appearance of being above personalities but were not.

What can be learned by beginning to examine the Interregnum and Restoration periods, and especially one region, under a magnifying glass? In one direction it shows how regional studies provide a reality check on the national narrative instead of remaining an appendage lost in parochial musings. Concentrating much of the narrative on Wiltshire proves especially informative, since part of national experience and the shaping of the whole Atlantic world began right here in mid-seventeenth century southern England. From the other direction the book insists that local studies ought not to shy away from big issues and scholarly modes of explanation. It is with this in mind that the final chapter in particular analyses the national economic growth that descended from the system set up or confirmed in the 1650s and 1660s. Interpreting this means stepping out of what might be called, in the cant term, the comfort zone of local history. This should seem obvious because there have long been detailed studies of local communities interested in the relationships of their social and economic structures to the national picture, especially the civil war. Notwithstanding this, typical histories continue to overlook or minimise the complicated and contradictory currents flowing in the provinces.

Chief among regional studies is the late Alan Everitt's Historical Association pamphlet of 1969, *The Local Community and the Great Rebellion*, in which county differences and loyalties were emphasised. Everitt struggles, as all writers on the period must struggle, with the tensions between old local allegiances, the intrusions of London money, and the disruptions of warfare. In many areas men remained fixated on their farming, as they had to be when the crucial margin of well-being depended on a good year. Small squires preferred to stay close to the land and ordinarily were not much disturbed by the fighting unless it loomed near. Everitt particularly chooses to contrast the introverted little cattle-rearing manors of Leicestershire with the great houses of Northamptonshire. It made a difference whether a county could be officered by great lords, as in Northamptonshire, or was dominated like Leicestershire by farmers who were dismissed by later Cavaliers as 'the female gentry of the smock.' Even among the larger landowners only a proportion lifted their eyes from the management of their estates before the eighteenth and nineteenth centuries.

Everitt points to the intense hold of local loyalties, instancing Mary Hyde, daughter of a Trowbridge clothier and mother of the Earl of Clarendon, who never once in her life stepped over the Wiltshire border into a neighbouring shire, despite for years residing within five miles of Gloucestershire. When people like Mary Hyde spoke of their 'country', says Everitt, 'they did not mean England, but Wiltshire or Kent, Leicestershire or Northamptonshire, Cumberland or Durham.' Generalisations are virtually defeated by the sheer variety of county experience. The highest common factor does not attain any great height. It is scarcely surprising, but not entirely realistic, that national histories are inclined to gloss over the intricacies. A national average may tell the rudiments of the tale but must remain an amalgam that cannot penetrate far into the conflicts and alliances of the time.

In the present book, the role of personal ambition is indicated, in order to temper institutional analysis by bringing individuals back in, which is to say reintroducing human agency. As the philosopher, William James, wrote, 'a large acquaintance with particulars makes us wiser than the possession of abstract formulas, however deep.' Tracing the webs of personal relationships in the countryside at any period would be an endless occupation and, although the present book confines itself to illustrative examples, what will become clear is that conventional impersonal history is insufficient. An eloquent passage quoted by Everitt from *Hodge and his Masters* by the incomparable late nineteenth-century Wiltshire writer, Richard Jefferies, comments on the intricate relationships of rural society. Moreover Jefferies was well aware that many of the reasons behind friendship or grudge were scarcely knowable: 'to get at the secret behind the speech, the private thought behind the vote, would occupy one for years.' A modern expression might be, 'you had to have been there.' Yet, important though personal connections were, concepts and categories from economics also remain essential if history is not to become aimless essay-writing – described by a natural scientist as the type of writing in which an author does not know when he starts where he will finish. What is needed is a joint humanistic and social science account.

Penruddock's little Royalist eruption was doomed yet, to widespread astonishment, the monarchy was restored within five years. Defeat had hit one side, then the other, until in 1660 the Restoration handed victory to the Royalists, although what then took place was not the winner-takes-all outcome familiar from continental wars. Retro-propaganda and cavalier triumphalism there were but the significance of the Restoration was as a rare 'elite settlement' in which gains were shared with those among the Puritan elite who had been instrumental in bringing it about. From the confusion of the times came the result that victors and vanquished came together again as a single landed class able to circumscribe royal authority and perpetuate their own power.

This was one of the world's great 'elite settlements' and is held to exemplify the peaceful nature of English society. Such settlements, for instance the classic case of Edo period Japan, are usually presented as deals between ruler and ruled, whereas the argument here is that in Restoration England there was an additional settlement between the factions of landowners who had fought one another during the Civil War. One pacifying element was the retreat of Puritanism from the politico-religious sphere to a narrower religious one. The fusion of the factions also established or re-established the increasingly repressive system of landed estates. Agriculture was the largest sector in the economy and a landowning class, unified in many ways, was to preside over it ever after.

Two very different authorities, the Marxist Christopher Hill and the American liberal, William E. Dodd, made grand claims for the endurance of the arrangements and policies of the mid-seventeenth century. They argued independently that Oliver Cromwell's 'reign' (Hill) or the first eight years of Charles II's reign (Dodd), that is to say about fifteen scarcely interrupted years in the 1650s and 1660s, set the course of English, even world, history for centuries. They did not however explain the fact of continuity and an explanation is called for because many types of disturbance may surely have deflected history from an easy passage down the years. An interpretation is needed in which each stage constrained and was replicated by the next, a process known as path dependence.

Charles II offered assurances that his would be a limited monarchy. The class that accepted this promise was refreshed in each subsequent period by new cohorts of money-makers from the City. The incomers quickly assimilated to prevailing landowner tastes, attitudes and exercise of power. They were drawn by the magnet of country estates; some of them were themselves the younger sons of landed families. Land offered status, amenity and access to political office, the power of which was often used to suppress further dissent, especially murmurings in favour of more equality like the Last Labourers' Revolt of 1830. Individual families might fall out of the charmed circle but they would be replaced by others who bought their estates, as by a homeostatic mechanism working blindly to ensure the continuity of the class as a whole. The surprising re-combination of the ruling Puritan and Royalist tiers is well illustrated by the case of Martin Noel, who served Cromwell's Protectorate but rapidly became one of the clique of 'interlocking directors' running the country under Charles II. Given the carryover between Republican and Royal rule there is no great need to choose between the Hill and Dodd accounts. Despite later political uncertainties, the 1650s and 1660s had already established the lineaments of the stability attributed to the fifty years after 1675 in J. H. Plumb's classic work, *The Growth of Political Stability in England, 1675-1725*

Some Cromwellian officers but many more of the foot soldiers continued to adhere to nonconformist sects that formed a not very plush alternative to the Anglican landed establishment. This sublimation of politics in religion is the subject of a chapter here. Once more the detail is drawn from Wiltshire and nearby counties. Two further chapters discuss the shocks which successive losers experienced and their responses to them, and the fusion of major Roundhead and Royalist landowners back into the domineering layer of society from which both had originated. George Orwell's label, 'Animal Farm', catches the spirit.

This caste supplied the personnel who ruled the countryside and in many ways the whole nation during the following centuries. They made sure to keep an ever-firmer grip on power and build up estates that became larger and larger. Descriptively there can be no doubt about the significance of the landed interest, which had torn itself apart in the Civil War but afterwards was never significantly challenged from within or without. Authority and conspicuous consumption went hand-in-hand at the expense of other dwellers in the countryside, which for a very long time meant most people in the realm. In large measure the estate system was an exercise in rent-seeking, with the landowners taking out more than they ever put in. Strictly speaking, a taste for rural living that was more marked than in continental countries needs its own explanation. Part of the impulse was high-grade consumerism, the attraction of owning an estate being so compelling. But that was true in many countries. Another part was the value and status that came from joining a network of immense influence. Perhaps the point was that landed ambition was less frustrated in England's relatively fluid social circumstances. The attraction persists, as witness the sumptuous new houses again being built in the twenty-first century countryside.

The over-arching place of the landed interest raises the larger issue of the role of institutions and social organisation in bringing about economic growth. Such matters should not be ignored, especially as local and regional history introduces a touch of realism into the analysis. There is no reason for local work to be purely descriptive, much less antiquarian. As to institutions, influential academics are currently of the opinion that in England they were special; more precisely the argument is that property rights were made secure by the accession of William of Orange in the Glorious Revolution of 1688. Prominent figures in economics assert that this led directly to economic growth and even industrialisation. It is repeated as a mantra, regardless of the century-long gap until the conventional beginning of the industrial revolution. This interpretation is not made true by the frequency with which it is asserted. It is just a means of cutting history's Gordian Knot.

A thoughtful case that English institutions were purposely and successfully designed is made by Douglas Allen. His position is ingenious and stoutly defended but this book cavasses the opposite, urging that the economy expanded through market growth despite institutional inadequacies and the costs they imposed. Property was never fully secure and property rights were open to challenge. The introduction of a land registry was repeatedly resisted by a legal profession that gained from the work involved in confirming ownership in the face of inconsistencies in the evidence. The recording of property rights is always prey to human failings.

As has been noted, much of the research on which this book is based was carried out in south-central England. This is because the investigation started with the Penruddock Rising and expanded through the personalities and places involved in it, where a source about one locality often helpfully led to another nearby. Concentrating close to where the Penruddock Rising began is useful for revealing the personal relationships without which history may become a dance of faceless marionettes. In any case, the central southern counties played a larger political role in the past than they do now. By contrast, 'national' studies tend to be diffuse, cherry-picking examples from across the country and ignoring the dense network of connections revealed by closer examination. Fortunately there is an alternative tradition of work on economic development, demonstrating its contingent, spontaneous, decentralised and barely predictable nature. The implication is that national development is the sum of countless stories of local development. This book weaves together a number of such episodes.

ACKNOWLEDGEMENTS

TWO KIND FRIENDS, John Anderson and Shaun Kenaelly, read the chapters as they were written and made all-too-pertinent comments, for which I am nevertheless most grateful. The same applies to my son, Christopher. Other friends supplied materials or accompanied me on exploratory visits, notably Alan Albery in Hampshire, Syd Flatman in Gloucestershire and Oxfordshire, and Michael and Pauline Tarrant in several counties, especially a memorable trip to East Anglia. Many other people helped, too, such as Douglas Allen of Simon Fraser University, Louis Sicking of Leiden University, John Chandler of the Victoria County History and local historians, museum curators and passers-by everywhere. I thank them here and above all thank my wife, Sylvia, who edited the book and accompanied me on innumerable visits to villages, churches and country houses. She had become accustomed to the procedure by a lifetime of excursions to post-seventeenth century landscapes and sites, and she bowed to my insistence that our holidays in Hampshire, Dorset and Suffolk be devoted one summer to tracking the spoor of John Penruddock, Francis Jones, and other figures back in the seventeenth century. That gave an enjoyable focus to our travels. I hope she agrees.

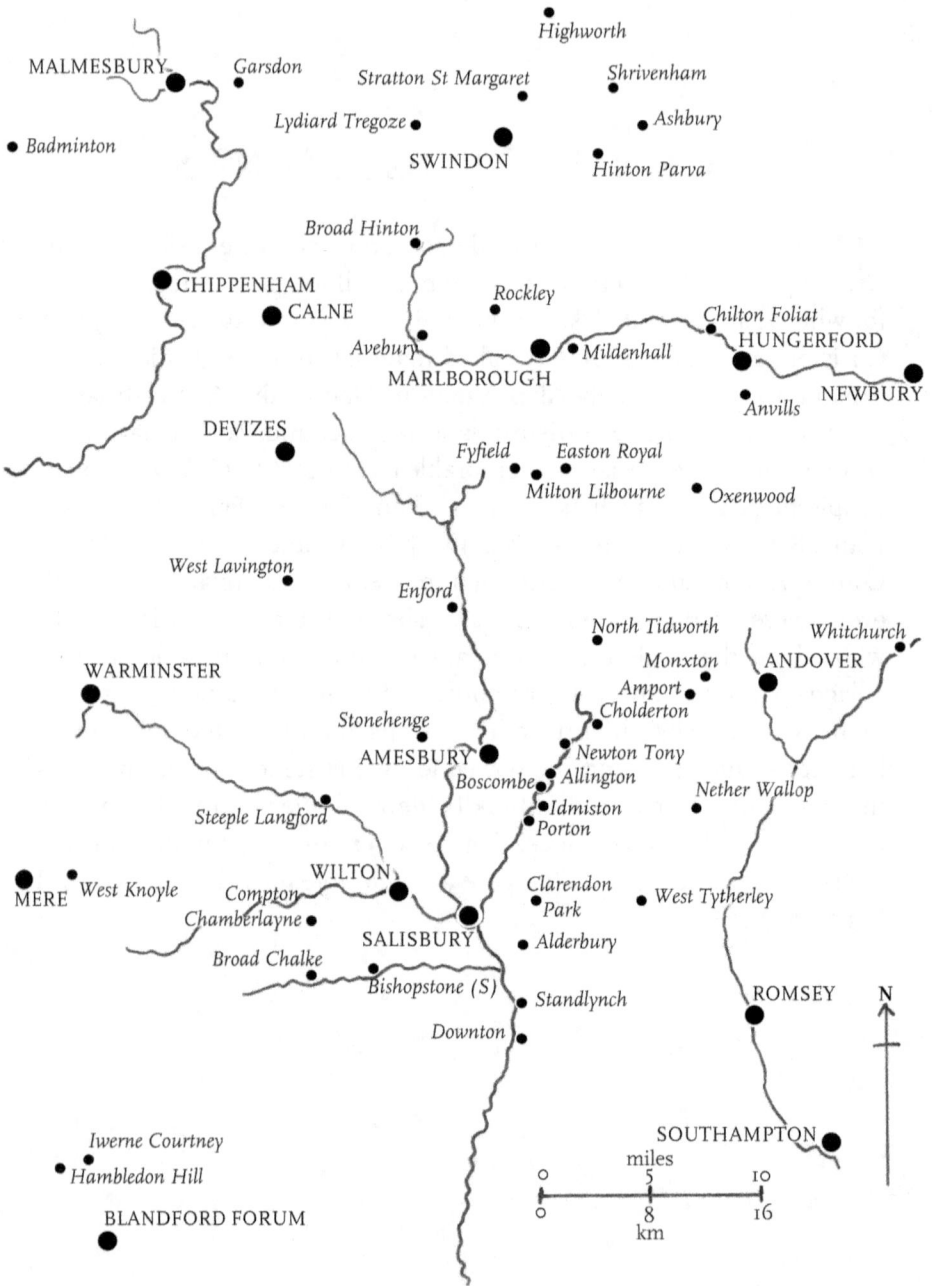

Map of the main places referred to in the text

I

SMALL EARTHQUAKE IN WILTSHIRE

Tʜᴇ ᴛʀᴏᴏᴘᴇʀs ꜰʀᴏᴍ Marlborough came to Easton for John Wildman in February, 1655. They crept up the stairs of his lodgings and found the door of the room ajar. Wildman was leaning his elbow on a table, dictating to a scribe, whom Milton would have called his amanuensis. Seizing the pair and a few weapons, the soldiers found that Wildman had been drawing up a manifesto beginning, 'The declaration of the free and well-affected people of England now in arms against the tyrant Oliver Cromwell.' Wildman was already being watched. He was a Leveller, far to the left of Protector Cromwell, yet plotting rebellion with men from the opposite end of the political spectrum, disaffected Wiltshire Royalists. From the Parliamentary point of view his machinations may genuinely have threatened the Protectorate, given the rumble of Royalist dissent in the country as a whole, the number of plotters arrested in January and February, and the fear that Levellers in the army might join in.

Cromwell read Wildman's manifesto, read it out to the City fathers in London, and committed its author to jail in Chepstow castle. But Wildman was out of jail the next year, having agreed to spy on the Royalists and so get his estates back. He was a mixture of life-long conspirator, opportunist and speculator in forfeited Royalist lands. In the early 1650s he had bought land in twenty counties, sometimes as an agent and sometimes on his own account. As Macaulay said of him, 'with Wildman's fanaticism was joined a tender care for his own safety. He had a wonderful skill in grazing the edge of treason...' and of the fact that he was made postmaster-general in 1689 Macaulay gave it as his opinion that this was 'for services no good man would have performed'. Wildman ended his life rich, ensconced in the Beckett estate at Shrivenham, Berkshire (now Oxfordshire) which he had bought from his Leveller friend, Henry Marten. After duplicity and escapades throughout his life, he was finally laid to rest in the church there in 1693, beneath a handsome slab of Purbeck marble that may still be seen.

At the start of 1655 Wildman had been in Easton, possibly lodging with a sequestered cavalier, Michael Clark, rather than in the big house belonging to the prominent Wiltshire family of Seymours, who at this time were doing their best to stay out of trouble. The details do not seem to be known but Easton, since called (indelibly but mistakenly) Easton Royal, was not as remote from the centre of affairs as that cul-de-sac of a village now appears. It was close to a south-north road not far from Marlborough, which was a significant Parliamentary town on an important east-west route. The Royalist, Sir Henry Moore, had planned to attack the town, a project hastily abandoned. The Levellers, too, had been thinking of rallying in the district. Moreover, Easton was merely twenty miles as the crow flies from the cathedral city of Salisbury and only half that distance from the valley of the Wiltshire Bourne from whose villages several of the conspirators in the Rising came.

Plotting is always complicated and obscure. Although we now have more of a bird's-eye view, the links are no easier to decipher than they were then – less so, because contemporaries at least recognised the names of their contemporaries and were familiar with places whose relative importance has long since altered. In 1655 Wildman undoubtedly knew something of the Royalist plan. He did not know quite enough however for the Cromwellians to stifle it, which they managed to do with threats in the Midlands about the same time, or he would have spilled more beans. Even so, he and other informants in the custody or under the thumb of Cromwell's spymaster, John Thurloe, were able to pass on sufficient hints to put the regime on the qui vive. This spurred it to be ready to mobilise fast and enabled the Roundheads to frustrate the Penruddock Rising almost as soon as it began. Guards had already been doubled at the ports and on 26th February, 1655, race meetings (where horsemen might congregate) were forbidden. Strangely, Cromwell did not think to forbid fox-hunts, which he had earlier done in Gloucestershire, and hunting was what the conspirators used as a cover for plotting. Even so the Protector was clearly rattled and the hopeful Royalists were rattled too. Under interrogation, Francis Jones, one of the three principals in the Rising and great-nephew of an ancestor of mine, told Cromwell and Thurloe, 'they were much troubled that Wyldman was taken.'

Penruddock's Rising is often passed over by historians as at best a footnote to history, Antonia Fraser being an honourable exception. The dismissal is not quite right. Failure it quickly was, going off half-cock. A minor episode in the roiling history of the seventeenth century it may have been. Yet its tremors were shocking at the time: an armed rebellion able to capture a cathedral city was no small matter. It was significant for four reasons. First, it persuaded Cromwell to establish military rule under the Major-Generals, something so un-English as to attract horrified attention then and ever after. Secondly, even before the Restoration of the Monarchy in 1660, it gave rise to a debate in the Commons about the enslavement of free-born Englishman, because two of the rebels who had been transported to the sugar plantations managed to get home and circulate a pamphlet exposing the chicanery of those who had bought and sold them. Thirdly, economic policies and the landed system that ruled rural England for centuries afterwards found a crucial ratification in the events and alliances that followed. Fourthly, the interest I find in the Rising because ancestral relatives of mine were involved is not exclusively personal indulgence: what happened to them and the district where they lived establishes an immediacy missing from standard histories.

The Rising, then, was a Royalist rebellion against the dour Roundhead regime so unloved in the countryside. The capture of Salisbury was alarming to people who thought political struggle had been ended by beheading Charles I in 1649 and replacing his rule by Parliament's, or as it turned out by that of the quasi-dictator, Oliver Cromwell. The prelude to the Rising had been two Civil Wars, the second more vicious than the first and far more destructive than English legend admits. The causes of the wars have resisted efforts by generations of historians to find a simple key but a difficult tangle of family connections played a bigger role than modern historians admit. It is enough to note here that Royalists loyal to Charles's exiled son, Charles II, were subject to exactions and humiliations that many were reluctant to bear. Revolt simmered and occasionally broke surface. The 1655 rising led by and named after the Wiltshire landowner, John Penruddock, was the most serious of these Cavalier outbursts.

The politics of the Interregnum, until Charles II was restored to the throne in 1660, were as intricate as those of any era and more complicated than most. Innumerable individuals were involved; identifying their blood connections requires detective work, and recalling

John Penruddock

their names, and remembering the names of the small villages whose manorial lords many of them were, makes the head spin. Genealogy introduces innumerable specifics. Political positions were stated, half-concealed, or amended; agitators agitated; the army squirmed when soldiers did not get their pay on time. Was the Cromwellian regime going to usher all men into equality and freedom or would it impose an ever more repressive Puritanism? In the prevailing uncertainty the Levellers, some of whom really did believe in equality and most of whom resented the way Cromwell had blocked the liberal Agreement of the People of 1649, were willing to temporise with the murmuring Royalists. Perhaps these extremes might merge into an upheaval big enough to unseat the regime. The conservative Royalists certainly hoped so. This was the point at which John Wildman appeared on the stage at Easton, only to be whisked away to jail, leaving Penruddock's Royalists to rise unaided.

John Penruddock was full of grievance, not least because two of his younger brothers had died fighting for the King. He was also one of the many landowners punished for their allegiance to the crown by fines meant to swell the Parliamentary coffers but designed in addition to limit resources that might be spent on revolt. Furthermore he had form as a leader of the Clubmen. The Clubmen are commonly presented as politically neutral and opposed to all plunderers, Cavalier or Roundhead. Much plundering did take place, at first because armies were expected to live off the land, but soon because some among them found theft too tempting. As one instance, a company of five soldiers passing up the Bourne valley towards Marlborough, 'being resisted by the owners of such poultry and other provisions as they took, they beat many very sorely and at Idmiston cut off the hand of one Nott...' To recognise the alarm such disorder caused, it scarcely matters which army was involved. Both stole and both committed atrocities, so that local people armed themselves and formed alliances to repel whichever soldiers were making trouble.

Yet the genesis of Clubmen resistance was not quite so straightforward. Its origin may after all not have lain in spontaneous gatherings of countrymen but in a fortuitous meeting between the Dorset landowner, Anthony Ashley Cooper, and a lawyer, Sergeant Fountain, at an inn in Hungerford. This was presumably the hamlet of that name on the edge of the New Forest, not far from Dorset, rather than the town of Hungerford, Berkshire, which has other claims to notice in the troubled history of the times. Cromwell became determined to suppress the Clubmen, which seemed to him dangerous armed gangs, particularly a large group defending the iron-age earthwork on Hambledon Hill, Dorset. He suspected they were crypto-Royalists, although they had killed marauding Royalist soldiers as well as Roundheads. He definitely did not want a 'third force' to emerge in the countryside, especially since (despite traditions of their spontaneity) these men were soon organised and officered by members of the clergy and landowner class.

The Dorset landowners among the leaders included John St Loe, whose family was intermarried with that of the later Penruddock conspirator, Francis Jones. St Loe was one of those selected to carry a petition from the Clubmen to the king at Oxford. He was afterwards to involve himself in the Penruddock Rising but dodged the consequences. General Fairfax, charged in 1645 with dealing with the Clubmen, found that when overcoming a large rabble of what Cromwell termed 'poor silly creatures' armed with clubs, pitchforks and scythes, he had also taken prisoner two gentlemen, John Penruddock of Compton Chamberlayne, Wiltshire, and John Fussell of Blandford, Dorset. They were released on their promise to desist from further activities of the sort. Ten years later Penruddock may be thought to have broken his word.

By the mid-1650s it was harder than ever to keep intentions of rebellion under wraps, although as a precaution the arrangements for the Penruddock Rising were withheld from some supporters until the last minute. Most of those involved tried to disguise their purpose behind screens of everyday activities and if they were known Royalists by pretending resigned acceptance of Roundhead rule. The difficulty of discovering their secret aims lay in the fact that they engaged in what is called preference falsification, whereby people conceal their true likes and intentions, as modern voters may do when badgered by pollsters. Seeing through such dissimulation is hard, especially in violent times when individuals have good reason to tell an enquirer what they think he wishes to hear. In these circumstances the usual methods for penetrating the fog - bribery, coercion and intercepting the mails - help only up to a point. Tricking individuals into revealing their true feelings is what is needed.

The Cromwellians found it hard to cope with faked preferences. Because many of them were ardent about their own beliefs, they swung nervously between convincing themselves that right-thinking people must agree with them and anxiety that enemies were lurking everywhere. Suspicion could extend to one's own supporters and Cromwell was said to have had a personal 'jealousy' that parliament had not disapproved of Gerard's 'design', which was a Royalist plot to assassinate him. He gave parliament's potential disloyalty as his reason for dissolving it. In the nineteenth century there was a famous disagreement between the historians, R. D. Palgrave and C. H. Firth, as to whether the Penruddock Rising was, as Palgrave contended, deliberately engineered by Cromwell via his spies and double-agents as an excuse to set up the dictatorship of Major-Generals. Firth pointed out that this was a beautiful hypothesis, philosopher's talk for something theoretically possible but for which there is no evidence. He argued that motives are not necessarily constitutional but reflect material forces, as if he were agreeing with Karl Marx.

On the surface the regime could learn something of what was going on via Spymaster Thurloe, who was good at 'turning' suspects and prisoners. Yet the fact that the Rising did get going shows that the regime was not omniscient. Afterwards Thurloe congratulated himself on the levies Cromwell raised quickly and persuaded himself that the mass of the population was not in favour of the house of Stuart, but how far he believed people were genuinely reconciled to the alternative offered by Cromwell is unclear. Counter-espionage was far from easy. One of Thurloe's predecessors, Elizabeth I's spy chief, forger and arch-dissimulator, Walsingham, offered a model of cold efficiency, since while it can never be certain how many smuggled Roman Catholic priests he failed to find, a creditable total of 471 was actually discovered, executed, jailed or banished. Inspired by this example, Thurloe's network of informers was kept busy, though it was less effective in the countryside than in the towns. Spying is never cheap; one modern estimate comes from a study of a very different society, Communist Lithuania, where surveillance cost the state 2 per cent of GDP. The cost can only be guessed in modern China, where 4 per cent of a population of 400,000 in one district were on the payroll of the security services. As Adam Smith might have put it, internal defence was greater than opulence.

The Royalists were as convinced as the Roundheads of their own rectitude and misled themselves in the opposite direction. Smarting from fines, impositions and interference by zealots – the gentry were sportsmen whose energies typically went into hunting and whose motto in other respects might have been 'pas trop de zele' - they were led to over-estimate disaffection with Puritan rule or at any rate willingness to risk rising against it. As is likely to happen to people in their situation, the conspirators spoke chiefly to one another or those they felt they could trust. Family members and friends appeared the most trustworthy and as a result of listening too much to the opinions and promises of these close circles the Royalists became over-optimistic.

The earlier defeat of the Clubmen may have contributed to the limited popular support for the Penruddock attempt, as may the fact that despite their political views the gentry found the revival of law, order and prosperity under Commonwealth and Protectorate unexpectedly congenial. Working people too may have calmed down by 1655, in which year, according to calculations by Thorold Rogers, the real wage peaked. As a post-Restoration bishop of Salisbury was to say, 'We always reckon those eight years of usurpation a time of great peace and prosperity.' This may have restricted rebellious behaviour to the most ardent among those inclined to the Royalist side.

Neither Cromwellians nor Royalists proved adept at reading between the lines. Whereas the Cromwellians misjudged the scale of active rebelliousness, the Royalists ended in dismay at the broken promises of sympathizers and the speed with which Penruddock's small force melted away. Both sides had too readily accepted assurances made to them, just as pollsters do when they fail to make correct predictions of the results of elections. A classic modern case where varied approaches were tried was that of East Germany. There, some of the methods were as devious as the false purposes which psychologists announce in order to mislead participants in experiments. Thurloe was devious too but he did not grasp the need for sampling and in any case lacked resources on the East German scale. He was a little off the mark and sensed the breeze in his day even less accurately, perhaps, than the East German Stasi did in theirs. Given what was at stake, this might have been fatal. For some Royalists, convinced there were plenty of 'masked royalists' waiting the call to arms, false hopes of support really were fatal.

They tried a preliminary foray. In February 1655 some of them began to canter towards the assizes town of Salisbury but finding that few joined them, turned homewards again. They also abandoned plans to assault Winchester because its garrison had been reinforced. An assault on Marlborough, with men hidden in carts ready to leap out and secure the horses at the inns before disarming the guards, was likewise abandoned. Something similar came to naught in Taunton. Notice the emphasis on horses, essential for transport, useful for communications and indispensable for a cavalry force. Cromwell, who was informed of the Rising the very day it took place, at once ordered the seizure of all horses in public stables in London and Westminster, as well as the delivery of all private stores of gunpowder to the Tower.

Cromwell's prior wariness had led the Royalists to advance Penruddock's Rising ahead of the proposed date of 18th April and make a start anyway, futile though it was likely to prove for a single regional force to chance a rebellion. An expectant, exiled, Charles II, 'privately came into Zealand ready to pass into England if the undertaking should be crowned with success', so an eighteenth-century *History of England* reported. He was tracked to Middelburg and Flushing by a Cromwellian agent who even discovered with whom he stayed at the former place, where it is disingenuously reported that the very young daughter of the house made his confinement 'more supportable.'

The *History of England* also announced that the rebels riding into Salisbury consisted of 'Penruddock, a Cornish gentleman with Jones, Grove and some others' at the head of two hundred mounted men. The litany of minor errors found in accounts of the Rising starts at this point and continues to this day. The first mistake is that John Penruddock was not Cornish, he was a member of a Cumbrian family well settled in Wiltshire. He was drawn into the affair by his cousin, Edward, a former six clerk (a post of the Court of Chancery). What is correct is that Penruddock, Hugh Grove and Francis Jones, with colonels' commissions from Charles II, were expecting to garner enough support to make each of their three separate troops up to regimental strength.

Conspiring Royalists in England often belonged to the main clan-
destine organisation, the Sealed Knot, but this had become anxious and
unwilling to move. Penruddock belonged to a rasher set called the Action
Party. The king had despatched from his continental exile a supposedly
jovial military man, Sir Joseph Wagstaffe, to command the enterprise.
Penruddock and his men on their horses met Wagstaffe at Clarendon
Park, close to Salisbury, and they all clattered into the city on 12th March.
Among them was Thomas Mompesson from Tidworth, whose forty
horsemen comprised the largest unit in a total force of 180 or 200.

Salisbury was taken by surprise and fell to the rebels. Their first
move was to secure all the horses they could find, though they sought
no other plunder. They took captive in their beds the judges who had
arrived for the assizes, one of whom was the Lord Chief Justice. They
also seized the High Sheriff of Wiltshire, John Dove, a man much
disliked for trafficking in forfeit lands. Although mishandled and
weeping, Dove was stubborn enough to refuse to proclaim Charles
II as King. Wagstaffe was eager to make a start by stringing up the
judges. Penruddock and the country gentlemen thought this cruel and
had the judges released, merely burning their commissions, an act of
clemency that was not admitted in their defence when they were tried.
At the Sheriff's house some resistance was offered by Major Henry
Wansey of Warminster, a Puritan watchmaker who paid dearly for his
views at the hands of a mob in his home town after the Restoration,
when the tables were turned yet again. There was no other resistance
in Salisbury but no welcome either.

The rebels were soon milling around, disappointed that the
inhabitants did not embrace them, which was less than astonishing
given that towns tended to be Puritan and this one had been badly
beaten up towards the end of the war. The culprits had been the Royalist
Northern Horse under Sir Marmaduke Langdale, whose troops acquired
an unsavoury reputation for plunder and rape in the Forest of Dean and
the Midlands. No great number of Salisbury recruits joined Penruddock's
party and few of those who did were local tradesmen. Once the affair
was safely over the city fathers, though frightened enough at the time,
were quick to refer to the rebels as 'a crew of desperate persons.' That
too was not surprising since the ranks had been swelled by setting free
common prisoners from the jail, including thieves in irons. Those who
joined were 'horsed' with the stolen nags. Penruddock may have had
rather better horses than men.

Individuals from several villages had started out to join Penruddock but turned back and never arrived. Gentry and their retainers from the surrounding region, especially recruits expected from Hampshire, were thin on the ground, whatever they may have promised. No stirrings at all were felt in Gloucestershire, possibly because of the inconvenient death the previous month of the sixth Baron Chandos, the only peer resident in that county. Sensing that his enterprise was in difficulty, and taking Dove along as a hostage, Penruddock set course for Downton and from there westwards across the downs by what in those times was a well-travelled track towards Blandford. And beyond, to Yeovil, where Dove was released. On again into Devonshire, where more of the adherents who had stayed the course as far as Yeovil now dropped away. Some who did come along broke ranks and scattered to Crewkerne, Chard and Dorchester, at which last place they forced open another jail and 'horsed' or mounted the jailbirds. The aim of the main body was to avoid the Parliamentary garrisons at Exeter and Taunton and make for Cornwall, where they thought another Royalist military force awaited. In the last resort there were small Cornish fishing ports from which they might sail away to join their king on the continent.

2

DEFEAT AND CAPTURE

A LL HOPES WERE dashed. Resting exhausted in the little town of South Molton in Devon, Penruddock and his men were attacked and soundly beaten by a single Roundhead troop. They could not match the professionalism of the New Model Army; as an underground movement they had had no chance of drilling together and those among them with military experience were out of date, the Civil war having ended ten years earlier. A few did manage to hold their attackers at bay for three hours by firing from the windows of their quarters but the Wiltshire principals were taken and imprisoned in Exeter jail. Other prominent figures succeeded in escaping, those who had come back from continental exile to join the Rising being quick to get away. Wagstaffe set his horse over a churchyard wall, crossed to St Malo and eventually turned up in Amsterdam. A goodly number of recruits from Wiltshire and Dorset had already deserted and still more slunk off in the night. Mompesson's forty horsemen from the Tidworth area had galloped away and did not figure among those taken. Some were less lucky and one of the Clark family who managed to flee to Herefordshire with a price of £100 on his head was later jailed twice simply for speaking in favour of Penruddock. His brother escaped but the frustrated Roundheads arrested their father, an old rector, and burned his fingers with match-cord, no doubt in the name of the Lord. He took six months to recover.

The troops of General Desborough, Cromwell's sycophantic brother-in-law, were soon sweeping the land for the fugitives. In the first blush of the search, while all was suspicion and confusion, the treatment of prisoners could be peremptory. Two of the 'Valiant Sixty' Quakers sent to proselytise southern England and unlikely to have been involved in any armed uprising were arrested in Honiton, Devon. Outside the chancel wall of the church at Bishopstone, South Wiltshire, are the marks made by large bullets 'exactly at the height of a man's head.' The legend

Dents made by bullets on the church wall at Bishopstone, South Wiltshire, where
followers of Penruddock are said to have been shot.

is that Penruddock's men were shot there. It may be that soldiers from
Marlborough under Major Boteler, whose troop had captured Wildman
and was now rushed across Salisbury Plain, were responsible. Similar
indentations can be seen in the West door, attributed more vaguely to
the execution of a soldier during the Civil War.

Other individuals were afterwards trapped in places well to the
west of Bishopstone but, said Desborough, 'very many of them doe
pretend to innocency'. One of the smallish number of landowners
involved, John St Loe, who had form as a Clubman, equivocated under
questioning and was not even tried. Desborough was discovering the
rule of which Hugh Trevor-Roper spoke in *The Last Days of Hitler*, that
'anyone who undertakes an enquiry of such a kind is soon made aware
of one important fact: the worthlessness of mere human testimony.'
Desborough did not care; lawyers might bother about niceties but he did
not. His response to the rebels, no doubt instructed by his father-in-law,
was a political one. Hence he did not trouble to take every suspect into
custody, especially the 'meaner sort.' Class terminology disfigures the
whole period, for example one of Penruddock's tenants was dismissed
as 'a person of no quality.' Common soldiers were little more than pawns

in the Rising, which from our distance in time can be seen as a struggle between factions of the gentry.

Desborough quickly felt he had more than enough prisoners (about 130) to make examples of or as he expressed it, 'to make a pattern for all the rest.' Any more to house and guard would have occupied too many of his men and exceeded the accommodation available at the inns. Moreover, if the prisoners were held together they would no longer be 'ignorant of each other's minds.' He felt that five or six key culprits should be dealt with first – John Penruddock, his cousin Edward Penruddock, Hugh Grove, [Robert] Duke of Stuckton, Hampshire, Francis Jones and John Jones. The Roundhead officer who had prevailed at South Molton was Unton Croke from an Oxfordshire legal family. He had previously accompanied the Cromwellian embassy to Sweden. During the Rising, Croke asked himself whether the Joneses were related, in other words was John kin to Francis. Yes, he thought correctly, 'the considerableness of the person guide me aright.' This does not mean they were big in stature but that John was a gentleman like his brother rather than a servant or one of the 'meaner sort'.

Ample detail began to emerge, interrogations and testimonies at the trials seeing to that. Penruddock's boast was that the officers who were captured were the ones who did not desert their men. He and Francis Jones were hauled up to London for more than one interrogation by Cromwell and Thurloe – we even know they were lodged in an inn at Charing Cross as more convenient for Whitehall than lodging them in the Tower. The victorious Roundheads afterwards sneered at the losers, one letter to Cromwell calling them 'this upstart crew.' Cromwell himself was contemptuous of the type of men who had rebelled. 'A company of mean fellows', he called them, which was not right given that seventeen were 'gentlemen' and many were respectable tradesmen. It cannot have gladdened his heart that congregations in the churches of London and round about prayed for them. The Protector may have scorned the opposition that had revealed itself but all the same he quickly tightened control of the country by the system of rule by Major-Generals.

The Attorney-General, Prideaux, said he could prove there was a rising but could not have told who were the principals, 'but by plowing with theire owne heyfars' – ploughing with their own heifers, meaning self-incriminating confessions. Penruddock and Jones claimed to have been rebelling for the liberties of the people, not on behalf of Charles II. No record survives of Penruddock's actual examination but he was scarcely repentant and having been returned to Exeter met his execution with fortitude. Francis Jones sang like a canary. His testimony survives among Thurloe's papers, although Thurloe already knew much of what he had to tell. The Clark Papers say that, 'His Highnesse was last night until 11 a clock upon examination of Colonel Penruddock and Colonel Jones, who were of Sir Joseph Wagstaff's party.' (Westminster, April 5, 1655). 'The examination of Francis Jones, taken the 4th of April 1655 [By Secretary Thurloe]' was printed in the mid-eighteenth century, using the linguistic forms and circumlocutions of the previous century that were already starting to seem archaic.

Francis Jones testified that he had gone to Boulogne a little before Christmas, 1654, to sell horses but fell in with English refugees, including the failed plotter Gerard, who spoke of 'designs' or conspiracies against the Protector. He was told a little more about the intended Penruddock Rising as the time approached, his informant being an apothecary called Pyle from Wallop in Hampshire who also had a London base. This seems to have been Richard Pyle, an old royalist agent in the West Country. Three days before the start Jones had been told the rendezvous and met Penruddock, Sir Joseph Wagstaffe and others there. Although they spoke bravely of simultaneous uprisings, as well as the prospect of the Levellers in the army joining them, those who eventually appeared were fewer than expected, 'and they were much troubled that Wyldman was taken.' Charles II was to land at Plymouth and once they had drawn the army away from London by the rising in the west and another in the north, there was also to be a rising in the capital 'and the parts about.'

When John Penruddock and Francis Jones were returned to jail in Exeter, Penruddock remained unrepentant but Jones was downcast: 'Colonel Jones seems to be a man of milder spirit, which often melteth into tears.' Other prisoners were less cowed and planned to break out of Exeter jail once Penruddock was back, but their little plan failed. Jones's subsequent letter to Thurloe from the jail on 2nd June survives. He had already confessed to his crime and to the aggravation of his offence through being related to his Highness, Oliver Cromwell, as we shall see. The letter grovels, speaks of the honour of gentlemen, and promises fidelity to the Protector ever after. 'I shall therefore humbly desire you to have a favourable opinion of me, and to continue your mediation to his highness for a pardon,' he ends by imploring Thurloe, 'by which you will most highly oblige me and my poore family to pray for his highness and your honour's prosperity, and ever remain Your honor's most faithfull and obedient servant, Francis Jones.' This is the language of simulated deference. Francis adds a footnote saying that his brother John, Captain John Jones, though too enfeebled by some months' imprisonment to write on his own behalf was willing to offer the same promise.

Francis Jones had bought their way out, to the fury of Sheriff Dove, who had a score to settle. Submissions will be made to 'His Highness' on behalf of some of the principals involved, wrote Dove, by reason of relations, 'but I am confident his highness will looke more upon the publique good, then there addresses...' He meant the Joneses should not evade the punishment meted out to the other leading figures simply because, as Dove knew, they were related to Cromwell.

Long-winded show trials took place at Exeter, Salisbury and Chard, Somerset. The treatment of the prisoners was rather haphazard. Education and social position helped to secure a hearing, though only up to a point. Procedural latitude had its limits and in the personalised way of the times the trials were corrupt, quite apart from the matter of stacked juries. The regime had not even managed to detain all of those adjudged guilty, so for the time being sentences on the absconders were for the record. Others who were in custody had already slipped the noose by turning 'Protector's evidence'. Sheriff Dove, always vengeful, assured Thurloe that no-one would be on the jury who was not of the right mind: 'The country is well searched for a panel this colour.' Penruddock put the bias to the test when he challenged 22 men before ever a jury could be sworn, although it did not save him in the end. Trials for treason were traditionally loaded against the accused. No counsel might appear for a prisoner except on a point of law, in other words there were to be no appeals to morality, whether sound, eloquent or anything else.

A junior counsel lamented that the principals in the affair were tried at Exeter, not at Salisbury where the affair had started and where a large and colourful assembly had gathered. No thought of impartial justice crossed his mind and as far as political leaders were then concerned, learnedness in the law and the wearing of fancy robes were ultimately close to play-acting. The judiciary did not gain its independence from Crown and government until the time of William III. But in an attempt to persuade the public of fairness, the Lord Chief Justice was present as an observer. Precisely how dispassionate he may have been is unclear since he was engaged at the time in wrangling with Croke to recover his horses, seized at Salisbury by Penruddock's men and confiscated in turn by Croke's soldiers. He did not get his horses but received compensation from public funds.

Chief of the commission was John Glynne, who had wisely avoided the trial of Charles I and despite his role in these trials ended up in the service of Charles II. Another of the commissioners had a less happy experience; he was John Lisle, a regicide who, when the tables turned in favour of the Royalists after the Restoration, was gunned down while leaving church in Lausanne. These opposite quirks of fortune illustrate the contingencies that prevailed in seventeenth century history. The lawyers strutted and indulged their professional casuistries. Proper formalities, as opposed to top-show, were observed only because some of the hand-picked jury proved obstinately independent after all. Yet the dispositions of the trials, savage in many respects, proved not invariably rigorous. Henry Clarke of Enford was tried for his life but to the fury of the attorney-general one of his relatives who was a barrister came down from London and got him off, though he was not released until the following year and then only on heavy bail. Christopher Willoughby of West Knoyle avoided punishment because of 'his advanced years' – he was sixty-one years of age. His son, who had organised the fox-hunting which had cloaked the conspiracy, also escaped conviction. In his case it was because the evidence offered against him was little more than that he had been seen beforehand riding around with a sword on a big horse. His submission was that he had ridden after the Cavaliers in order to persuade his brother-in-law to return. As Desborough had found, 'they doe pretend to innocency.'

The Willoughby manor house, West Knoyle, Wiltshire, where the plotters 'danced to a fiddler'

Beheading of John Penruddock from an old print

Yet Penruddock and Grove were beheaded and Jones was hanged, so declared the eighteenth-century history already mentioned, though it covered itself by a footnote admitting that 'some say' Jones was reprieved. He was indeed reprieved, at the Protector's express command. On the face of things this was an unlikely act of mercy merely for telling all, which other prisoners had been equally quick to do, and especially in view of the fact that he had been indicted and found guilty of High Treason.

From many historical accounts Francis Jones and his brother thereafter vanish, as if in a puff of smoke. They were among that part of the lesser gentry who were obliged to sell their land (usually because of debts and fines) and moved into the towns, or went overseas, or sank in the social scale. Anthony Wagner gives Derbyshire instances in *Pedigree and Progress*. Because few sources thereafter mention the Joneses, subsequent historians, copying from one to another, enquire no further. These Joneses do not figure in the ranks of later Wiltshire gentry and supply no more documents, unlike the descendants of Penruddock and Grove, whose families continued to be influential among the county's landowners for centuries. Having an ancestor who had been beheaded for rebelling in favour of the king was a cachet in the monarchical Britain re-established at the Restoration. On the other hand the very name of Jones, tainted as it was by escaping punishment at the hands of a Cromwellian tribunal, must have been an embarrassment to historians of a Royalist bent.

Penruddock was beheaded and his family paid seven pounds for the body to be fetched from Exeter for burial in his home church, where it was unearthed by proud descendants, minus the head, in 1855. His execution is boldly proclaimed on a board listing the deaths

JOAN Wife of JOHN CLARKE Efq! May 1622
LADY PENRUDDOCKE   Dec! 1630   by
JOHN PENRUDDOCKE   Dec! 1639   MONUI
THOMAS Son of JOHN PENRUDDOCKE an Inf! Dec! 1646 WYNDH
S! JOHN PENRUDDOCKE K! and   CHA
        DAME JOAN HIS WIFE June 1648   HENRIE
THOMAS PENRUDDOCKE   Aug! 1649   CHARLE
JOHN PENRUDDOCKE BEHEADED at   FRANCE.
        EXETER THE SIXTEENTH AND   ANNE H
        BURIED THE NINETEENTH OF May 1655
GEORGE SON OF JOHN and   HENRIE
ARUNDELL PENRUDDOCKE Sep! 1664 ANNE HE
JOHN an Inf! SON OF THOMAS and   M/
    FRANCES PENRUDDOCKE Mar! 1676 J.H. PE
EDWARD an Inf! SON OF THOMAS and
    FRANCES PENRUDDOCKE Jan! 1680 JOHN H
IANE an Inf! Daughter of THOMAS and

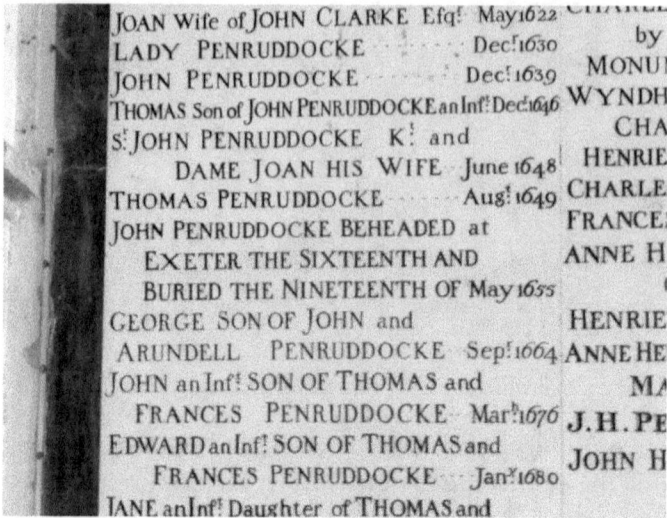

*Family board in Compton Chamberlayne church, Wiltshire, recording Penruddock's
beheading.*

of the generations of Penruddocks who held Compton Chamberlayne
until the 1930s. They owned the lace cap in which John Penruddock
was executed, stained and marred by the headman's axe. In Victorian
times related items were shown to the new Wiltshire Archaeological
Society when the carriages of members made their way to a meeting
at Compton Chamberlayne. One Penruddock became President of the
Society, so well established was the family, though attachment to the
Stuarts had lingered among them for a long time and an eighteenth-
century descendant used to join other Jacobites in the Cribbage Hut at
Sutton Mandeville, near Compton Chamberlayne, to drink the health of
the 'King over the Water'. As for Hugh Grove, the eighteenth-century
floor plaque to his grandson in Mere church proudly records that the
grandfather had been beheaded at Exeter in 1655, 'pro Rege et Lege'. In
the nineteenth century the well-heeled Grove family was as happy as
the Penruddocks to display memorabilia to the Wiltshire Archaeological
Society.

Beheading was seen as an act of clemency, likely to be granted to
gentlemen despite their crimes. If the executioner's axe were not too
blunt, death was instantaneous. By contrast hanging English-style was
barbarous, being death by strangulation and sometimes involving prior
drawing and quartering. This meant that near-strangulation was followed
by disembowelling and the burning of inner and private parts before

the victim's own dimming sight. Authorities differ about the number of Penruddock prisoners who were hanged. There are lists of names and although some suffer from the idiosyncrasies of seventeenth-century spelling (Mompesson appears in a list of suspects as Mumparsons) they ought to be sufficient for identification. Yet the records still vary and some authorities assert it is impossible to be sure of all who really were executed.

The vagaries of procedure mean that no obvious pattern emerges from the trials. Old sources report that seven rebels were hanged in Salisbury at the same time as the execution of a witch. The modern response to the executions and associated torture is not infrequently that they were simply what the times were like and those involved cannot be blamed for the horrors. This is the *autres temps, autres moeurs* defence, urging that all there is to say is that the past is another country. It will not wash when contemporaries can be found, as they can, who deplored and resisted the cruelty at the time.

The Penruddock trials were obviously at base political. Despite the fraught times, the law retained some use in supplementing the bullet or the hangman's axe and remained a normal instrument for resolving disputes. The constable of Speenhamland, Berkshire, was actually sued by their aggrieved owners for having conscripted horses in the service of the state during the Rising. A little more than a veneer of legalism suffused the trials themselves. Although the law was corrupt and idiosyncratic, it would nevertheless be too facile to dwell only on its class nature, then or later. Obviously individuals with deep pockets could fight cases beyond the reach of ordinary men and no one can dispute the structural injustice of that type, which continues to the present day. Yet judges were not solely creatures of the establishment. They were capable of putting legal form first, of delighting to play their sonorous legalistic games.

After the Restoration the compass needle naturally swung to the opposite quarter and the surviving Penruddock prisoners might actually find themselves rewarded, though not generously. In Dorset, little Puddletown and Beaminster, the latter a Parliamentary town, felt obliged to give each resident who had joined the Rising a little money. But by then about seventy luckless prisoners had been transported to Barbados. This was called 'Barbadoeing' or being 'Barbadozzed'. They were the ones who had been induced to plead guilty and so escape capital punishment only to suffer a verdict that might have been thought a fate worse than death. A few who had actually been acquitted were still transported! They had all been sold to merchants who shipped them out for resale to the owners of sugar plantations. In Barbados, unless they had connections or could buy their way out, they were effectively slaves, ill-treated and worse fed; Robert Duke died there. Hundreds of Royalist supporters, mostly Scots taken prisoner after the battles of Worcester and Dunbar, had already found themselves transported to Barbados. Some Scots were even sent to the Venetian Republic. The trade out of Bristol was big enough to satiate the slave market and bring it to a standstill. Small wonder, then, that John Adams and Thomas Jefferson visited Worcester in the 1780s on a pilgrimage to the place where they conceived that men had fought for and lost their liberties in 1651. The one bright spot in the history of transportation at this period is that sailors were reluctant to have their ships carry Quakers, who (on the basis of coincidences not then understood to be chance) were reputed to bring ill luck on any who persecuted them.

After the Rising, status might still count and in 1656 George Duke and Edward Penruddock (John Penruddock's cousin) petitioned to be sent from Exeter prison to Virginia rather than to Barbados. It is not astonishing that they wished to go to Virginia since it was almost a Royalist colony. There, despite the disgusting treatment of slaves who happened to be black, white men involved in the Rising had some hope of being welcomed. What is surprising is that the Cromwellian regime granted their request but perhaps bribes were paid. Edward and George got back to England by 1659 but Edward was arrested again as a precaution ahead of Sir George Booth's Cheshire rising in that year.

When they landed there in 1656, the unfortunates who were sent to Barbados were sold as the goods and chattels of Martin Noel, described as a London scrivener, i.e. notary and money-lender, Thomas Aherne, who was a London merchant originally from Herefordshire, and Captain Henry Hatsell, naval commissioner at Plymouth and an ardent Parliamentarian who got himself into a lot of trouble after the Restoration. Noel, the most prominent of the traders, almost came a cropper too. Among his victims was Marcellus Rivers from Binstead in east Hampshire. Rivers was a gentleman, literate and not without connections back home. At the trial he had pleaded on his own behalf and that of others, using the argument advanced by Penruddock himself, which was that since Cromwell was not in fact king their actions were not treasonable by definition. It did not prevail. Ironically, Rivers had not taken part in the Rising in person, though it is true he had been in the royal army until 1644. He was charged instead with running guns for Charles II.

After a year in jail, Rivers and others were hauled out of Plymouth, placed on shipboard without being told the destination, and locked below decks with the horses. Having succeeded in getting back to England, he published a pamphlet in 1659 together with a fellow returnee, Oxenbridge Foyle, complaining of the treatment they had received when working in the cane for the planters to whom Noel had sold them. Their price had been set at 1550 lb of sugar more or less, according to their 'working faculties'. The pamphlet was *England's Slavery, or Barbados Merchandise,* tellingly or sarcastically advertised as 'printed in the eleventh year of England's liberty, 1659'. Their treatment had been savage, though not as bestial as that meted out to black slaves, even in Virginia, where in a colony boasting great plantation libraries, any slave who was caught trying to learn to write risked having a finger amputated!

Rivers's case sparked a parliamentary debate about slavery in the very year of his return to England, that is to say even before the Restoration, but the Commons dwelt less on the iniquity of slavery in general than on whether free-born Englishmen might be enslaved, something condemned by both Republicans and Royalists. Unhappily this failed to prevent West Country prisoners from being transported after the Monmouth Rebellion of 1685, another Stuart revolt. Nevertheless the Penruddock Rising had at least prompted a significant debate on slavery, the law and the constitution. The debate took place despite the presence of Cromwellian members of parliament with much to hide and illustrates the complexities of a society wrestling with the ambiguities of power. Martin Noel's defence was disingenuous, claiming that the House had been misled and Barbados was in reality something like a West Indies beach resort. In 1660 Rivers tried to have him exempted from Charles II's amnesty for Cromwellians but that did not work either; far from it, Noel was useful to the king as a financier and instead of punishment he received a knighthood. Two or three years later his eldest son was likewise knighted. One might say the wicked flourish like the green bay tree.

Martin Noel was an enigmatic figure of whom it has been said, 'so widespread and varied were his activities that it may plausibly be suggested that for many years he was the most influential individual in England.' This is a bold claim and may be an exaggeration – how could one tell? – but cannot be far off the mark. If even approximately true, two conclusions follow. First, a biography of Noel, could enough material be found, would expose the tight nexus of individuals who dominated public and commercial finance in the 1650s. And not only in the 1650s: this nexus, once its members had helped engineer the return of the Monarchy, carried Cromwellian policies into the restored reign and helped to seal the prolonged dominance of aristocrats and squires.

Secondly, to find that such a major figure in a much-studied period is not mentioned in most histories is astonishing. Noel barely breaks the surface of the historical record, receiving only glancing allusions when he is discussed at all and no proper entry in the *Dictionary of National Biography* (the *History of Parliament* has not got around to the period). Given his power, he was remarkably self-effacing but was a personal friend of the most influential people, such as Anthony Ashley Cooper and the Cromwells. He had been one of those who favoured crowning Oliver Cromwell. Noel was Thurloe's brother-in-law and partner. It was through Noel that General Monck, who steered the Restoration of Charles II once the generals of the New Model Army had fallen out among themselves, stayed in constant communication with Thurloe.

Noel is scarcely known to historians (Antonia Fraser, the Canadian Gilbert Farthing and the American William E. Dodd being the main exceptions), other than as the founder of some almshouses in Stafford. This local act of largesse was one he could afford, though there is a hint that the bequest was never made complete due to losses he sustained at sea. He became Member of Parliament for Stafford and the fragment of his reputation which is noticed there has been sanitised in the Borough Council's town trail, which blandly announces that he 'invested in the colonies.' In reality he had his finger in every conceivable financial and commercial pie at home and abroad. In 1657 he was even made a committee member of the East India Company, with which formerly he had been in competition. Accordingly there is no great surprise in that the very same year he was pressing Cromwell to extend the Company's monopoly.

Noel was the greatest salt-master in the country and dealt in cotton and munitions, though his fortune, dispersed and concealed in every which way, proved virtually untraceable after his death. It was a web of financial interests and options, and like a spider's web revealed at one and the same time complex construction, tensile strength and insubstantial appearance. How much of it was a mirage is not clear from published sources. And from having been close to Cromwell, he moved to join the cronies of Charles II, of whom it is said (by Dodd) that there was 'rarely a group of leaders who so seriously shifted the course of modern history as did the little clique who surrounded Charles II from the summer of 1660 to the autumn of 1667.' In effect they held interlocking directorates on the ruling boards of the realm. 'Every important political and economic interest of Restoration England was thus under the control of eight intimates of His Majesty.'

Noel's case shows that, despite endless studies of the seventeenth century, there are still gaps in our grasp of how polity, society and economy worked, let alone how it was that the ambitions of leading figures among the Puritan elite came to be realised at the Restoration. In later chapters we shall try to fill a few of the gaps. As for the Penruddock Rising, which had given Noel one of his infinite opportunities for making a profit, Clarendon wrote in his history of the times that, 'this little fire, which probably might have kindled and inflamed the Kingdom, was for the present extinguished.'

3
MEMORIALS OF THE SEVENTEENTH CENTURY

MUCH IS MADE of the brother-against-brother aspects of the Civil war, which is not surprising since birth order and inheritance could shape political and religious affiliations. Besides this, who knows what incompatibilities of personality and jealousies about inheritance may have put relatives at one another's throats? When Oliver was attempting to stop Cambridge college plate heading to the court his own cousin turned out for the King. Only rarely will the source of personal differences and antagonisms surface in the documents. Nevertheless, loyalties were much more often respected and all members of a family typically supported the same side. Family ties figured strongly in recruitment by Penruddock. The conspirators were often related – to cite a single example, Maurice Bockland of Standlynch was married to John Penruddock's third daughter. There were scores of similar connections. Families tended to be large, often ten or twelve children, which opened the way for a cat's cradle of marriage alliances. Family connections were commercially important too, especially to younger sons who were excluded from the estate by primogeniture, meaning that the eldest son was the one who inherited the land, leaving his brothers and sisters to make their own way. Blood relationships, however distant, offered contacts in trading and professional communities as far afield as the then-favoured honeypots of Virginia and the West Indies.

The alternative to family and neighbourly relationships as explanations of political affiliations would presumably be to claim that allegiance arose out of pure intellectual choice. This would imply that people sat down, floating free of inherited attitudes or attachments to their kin, to reason their way towards whom to support. Not so: Everitt observes that few actions in the seventeenth century were determined, 'by unfettered idealism, or by abstract principle alone.' Mundane considerations intruded and although there were spectacular cases of falling out, the bonds of family were normally tighter as well as wider than they are today. The issue of those connections surfaces in later Stuart history, where a scholar arguing that politics was animated by personal relationships rather than party affiliation was subjected to attacks described by observers as downright vicious. That unedifying dispute may be disregarded here as irrelevant to the mid-seventeenth century, when the concept of 'party' was even more anachronistic. Admittedly, asserting the prevalence of family and local ties describes allegiances without entirely explaining them. How did the whole group or the patriarch originally decide where loyalty should be placed? Important as family relationships were, they hint at rather than fully elucidate political choices, which they influenced strongly rather than determined absolutely. Preference falsification was no doubt sometimes present. With occasional family members falling out with others and opportunists turning their coats, we seldom know with full certainty why individual people chose King or Parliament or (more rarely) managed to stand aloof.

Ancestral ties and the marriages of forebears were live parts of regional memory. In the absence of great need to switch around among one's associates, connections were cherished over the generations, particularly among those whose country seats were within a day's ride of one another. When transportation was restricted to horses, propinquity mattered more than it does today. Shared pastimes brought people together and at the sporting events of rural communities lay a good chance of discerning who sympathised with which cause. In a slowly changing society incomers soon attached themselves to its established webs of connection. One of the Penruddock conspirators avoided punishment because he had been at school with one of the judges. Membership in private bodies features in modern England too but nowadays there are more impersonal institutions with established rules that go a little further towards promoting on merit, breaking up of patronage and diluting of what in the seventeenth century used to amount almost to tribalism.

The thinking behind political choice may be documented in a few cases, though not for any sample that might seem representative. An alternative approach might be through what is called prosopography, which means determining the common characteristics of a group by making a collective study of the lives of members whose individual biographies are hard to trace. Allusions in this book to the origins and social connections of royalist rebels largely take this form. They give context to such biographies as are individually recorded and paper over the unavoidable cracks of the ones that are missing. Beyond this indirect approach, we need to seek what clues we can find in genealogy, which deals with traceable relationships within families rather than in the group. Fortunately we can assemble some information about the relationships of Francis Jones, the third man among the Penruddock principals and the one to escape beheading. Although the sources are incomplete and obscure, some of his background can be unearthed and his link to Oliver Cromwell exposed. We will turn to the detail in the next chapter in order to throw light on the inner workings of seventeenth-century society.

Among the families of Joneses related to Francis, the name of the first-born son mostly alternated between William and John, which makes for one of the difficulties in tracing the relationships. Family conventions of that sort were not unusual. Yet although personal names may have been stereotyped, place names were far from standardised. Obscurities and confusions abound, for instance Tytherley may appear in as distant a form as 'Tudeley'. The Wiltshire Mildenhall, which was the home village of the senior branch of the Jones family, has long been known as 'Minal' to distinguish it from Mildenhall in Suffolk and I shall use Minal wherever possible here. Like the two Mildenhalls, other pairs of place names dog the researcher: there are Bishopstones in north and south Wiltshire, Hungerfords in Berkshire and Hampshire, and Upwoods in Dorset and Huntingdonshire. Repetitions even occur in more than one country. Charles II waited at Flushing (Vlissingen) to hear the outcome of Penruddock's Rising and after the Restoration he bestowed the rights of the ferry to Flushing on one of his supporters - but this proves to have been Flushing in Cornwall, which (to pile on the complexity) had received its name in the seventeenth century at the hands of Dutch immigrants from Vlissingen who built three quays there.

On the other hand it does help in setting the scene that so many physical traces of the mid-seventeenth century are to be found, fragmentary and overshadowed by later monuments though they often are. 'Remnants of History, which have escaped the shipwreck of time', Francis Bacon called them in that same period. Their escape has occasionally been narrow, the statue of Charles II from 1661 in central Gloucester being one that was removed in the eighteenth century and not re-erected until 1945 – in a much more out-of-the-way place. It was by no means the only effigy of Charles to suffer such a fate. More sheltered remains from Bacon's day nevertheless do succeed in making seventeenth-century events seem concrete, though the metaphor itself is scarcely appropriate.

Churches contain plenty of ledgers (floor slabs), plaques and effigies from the Civil War period. Black marble ledgers, often with intricately carved heraldic crests, lie half under the altar or beneath lengths of damp carpet. Some stones are worn by the tread of ages but others remain sharply incised. All may be obscured by discarded furnishings, heavy pews or unwanted scenery from last year's nativity play. Many churches care for them no more than they do for other items such as the occasional torn old bibles left lying about or the gravestones in the churchyards, where natural history trumps human history and sculptures moulder in vegetation left rank because a lack of willing mowers means cemeteries are passed off as nature reserves. Failure to look after church possessions is not new and it is astonishing that so many of them do survive. The church guide for Haslingfield, Cambridgeshire, quotes a report of 1844 that says, 'the church has suffered considerably from neglect; the state of the floor at the west end of the north aisle is such as would certainly not be permitted in any gentleman's stable...' It was the Victorians and their immediate successors who tidied things up, kept them clean and could readily find village women to polish the brass.

In any church, memorials jostle for prime positions near the altar, just as the box tombs of yeomen farmers crowd for precedence outside the south door and avoid the 'devil's door' on the north. At least memorials inside the church are preserved from the weather. They celebrate the first member of some well-to-do family to arrive in the parish and buy the manor. He was draper of London, wine-merchant of London, linen draper of London, or some such, and had commonly been a younger son of a gentry family whose land went to the eldest son, obliging his brothers to enter the law, the church, the army or trade. Later plaques celebrate successive descendants of the founding father and the lineages, ranks and worldly achievements of those marrying into his line, all of them immortalised in virtuous epitaphs whose every goose is a swan.

There thus follow generations of generals, admirals, government functionaries, colonial administrators and above all incumbents ('thirty years vicar of this parish'). The memorials cite medals, honours, degrees and Oxford fellowships, each as if in some celestial curriculum vitae. Then the heir dies in a colonial field or goes down with his ship, another aspiring family buys the big house and the cycle revolves again. A proportion of the memorials are in Latin but village schools did not teach Latin. Entry to this level of society was not for the common herd and the talents of the sons of ordinary folk, never mind their daughters, were spurned from the start. The Cromwellian Protectorate moved away from using Latin in official documents but after the Restoration Latin returned. Never mind any rationalisations, the purpose, or latent function, was to keep the hobbledehoys for ever at arm's length.

Often enough the memorials present family trees, beautifully parodied by Nancy Mitford in *Love in a Cold Climate*. A real one at Coln St Denis, Gloucestershire, is a classic. It celebrates Sir Benjamin Kemp, Bart., who died in 1777, and reads in part that, 'He was the only Son left of a Numerous Progeny of Sir Robert Kemp Bart of Gissing, Norfolk, by his second Lady, a Miss Brand. But the Family Seat is now at Ubbeston in Suffolk.' The Robert Kemp commemorated had four wives and fifteen children but the title descended to a cousin and the estate to a niece. The 'marble' was erected by his only surviving sister, Mrs Shorte of Sevenoaks, Kent, relict of Darell Shorte Esq of Wadhurst, Sussex. The emphasis on property could scarcely have been bettered by Jane Austen. Notice that one of the wives was described condescendingly as 'a Miss Brand.' At least she had met her Mr Darcy.

Less conspicuous among the stone curricula vitae are those of Tudor and Stuart times, which tend to be squeezed between the full length effigies of medieval knights in armour and the panoplies of Georgian and Victorian self-congratulation. Nevertheless they spring out once they have caught the eye. The plaques and ledgers of men caught up in the Civil War and Commonwealth periods or their immediate descendants are still to be found if one is not above shifting furniture. After 1660, Royalist landowning dynasties were again quick to commemorate themselves. At Compton Chamberlayne John Penruddock's own memorial is unmissable. A large board in the church lists the successive heads of the family, if that is not too unfortunate a phrase given that it boldly announces John's beheading – a safe boast once the monarchy had been restored.

Memorial to Lawrence Washington, Garsdon, Wiltshire, taken through a broken windowpane of the locked church. A bounty hunter paired his son with John Jones as two Royalists ripe for fines.

Searching the churches of half-a-dozen counties reveals the wealth and dominance of landed proprietors. The memorial of 1643 for Sir Lawrence Washington is at Garsdon, Malmesbury, Wiltshire, where the church is kept locked but the monument can be glimpsed through a broken window pane. Sir Lawrence was remembered as one 'whom it pleased God to take into his peace, from the fury of the insuing Warrs.' In 1649 his son, also Lawrence, was paired with John Jones of Newton Tony, also in Wiltshire, as ripe for a Parliamentary fine. The elaborate memorials of the Ashley Coopers, family of the great turncoat, over-awe at Wimborne St Giles. John Wildman's ledger at Shrivenham is smart enough, despite his will asking as a memorial only 'some stone, of small price.' Perhaps black marble is what he meant. The family ledgers of his friend, the regicide Henry Marten, are obscured beneath matting a few miles away at Longworth, though Marten himself lies at Chepstow. Charles II had him imprisoned for life in Chepstow Castle but his freedom to dine with families round about was curtailed when he said he would take the same political course again. Ledgers at Quenington, Gloucestershire, for the kinsfolk of the regicide, Henry

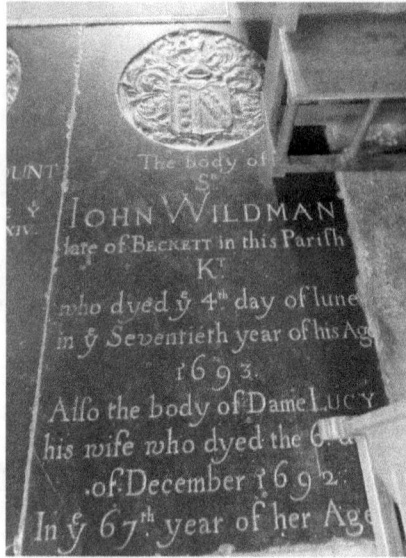

John Wildman's gravestone, Shrivenham, Berkshire (now Oxfordshire)

Ireton, are concealed by rich carpet along the aisle rather than mere matting. Memorials to members of the Hungerford family of about the same period are in places such as Black Bourton, Oxfordshire, and at Hungerford (Berkshire) itself.

Elaborate monuments to Wiltshire cavaliers who served in the war stand in the churches at Broad Hinton and Lydiard Tregoze. Royalist plaques can wax rueful about losses, especially of property, or about the sacking of the church itself, for instance at Stretton Grandison, Herefordshire. Ashbury church, Oxfordshire (formerly Berkshire), contains an ecstatic verse about a man who huzza'd the Restoration; while only two villages away at Hinton Parva another ledger records the death of a Parliamentary officer – guardedly because in truth he hailed from a Royalist family. In what may seem a supreme irony, plaques to the arch-Puritan Fiennes family are in good order in the church at Newton Tony. At first sight this is incongruous, given that they were fined for holding a nonconformist conventicle in their house. Status however trumped ideology. In any case, Cromwell's crony Nathaniel Fiennes had played just enough of a role by contemplating the return of Charles II at the start of 1660 to save himself from having to sue for pardon at the Restoration. Nevertheless Fiennes had been quick to retire to the country.

4
THE THIRD MAN

A FTER LOSING THE battle of Worcester in 1651, Charles II fled. He spent one day of his flight with Robin Phillips on the downs near Stonehenge and passed some of the time counting the stones. Phelips then handed the royal personage on to the next guide, Dr Henchman, in the fields near Heale House, which had a priest's hole where the king might hide. Afterwards Phillips 'rode that evening, leading the horse his majesty had rode, to his most faythfull friend Mr Jones his house at Newton-Tony'. This was north of Salisbury and nine miles from Heale, and was where the horse was to be stabled until the king needed it. In the event, the king did not require his mount again because he was eventually slipped across by boat from Sussex to France. He was to want no English horse until he returned in triumph for his Restoration in 1660.

Mr Jones was Francis Jones, one of the three principals in the Penruddock Rising of 1655. The three of them were in it together and the question is how did Jones avoid the executioner's axe that fell on the others, especially as the High Sheriff of Wiltshire was baying for his blood? Francis was of the minor gentry but the family afterwards sank below that status, leaving almost no later documents. Because it does not find much of a place in the historical record and because references to any one individual called Jones are endlessly difficult to disentangle from all the others, questions about Francis's must be approached elliptically. Indeed, if a man may be known by his friends, his associates in the earlier escape of Charles II after Worcester fight offer the best clues to his temperament.

According to Richard Ollard's book on the king's escape, Henchman and Phillips had the usual background of country gentlemen who had been educated at Oxford. In reality Henchman was a Cambridge man who had been ejected as canon of Salisbury, joined the Royalist forces and found his estate confiscated and library destroyed. At the Restoration he became Bishop of Salisbury. Robin Phillips was a younger son of the family who owned Montacute House, Somerset, though the heavy fines imposed on them as Royalists obliged him to live in Salisbury. Phelips certainly had been at Oxford, matriculating at Wadham College in 1634 aged 15. Francis Jones does not appear in *Alumni Oxonienses,* though one of his relatives, possibly his father, had matriculated at Hart Hall before going on to study law at the Middle Temple in the way gentry sons then did. The Middle Temple was the one among the Inns of Court most favoured by lesser gentry from the central southern counties. Francis's brother John had been admitted to the Middle Temple, as had another John Jones from Minal.

These men belonged, writes Ollard, 'to that section of the Royalist party, serious, educated, devout, its mainstay in the storm of war, whose natural leaders were Falkland, Clarendon and Ormonde, men whom Charles I did not favour until he was forced to nor Charles II retain when he felt free to let them go.' Because Phillips and Henchman were Francis's close friends we may assume he shared their attitudes. They were both richly rewarded at the Restoration because, although Charles II was not always a generous man and was without infinite resources when he came to the throne, he did lavish gratitude on those who had helped him during his desperate escape. It was an episode that stayed forever in the royal mind. Henchman was elevated to a bishopric, while Phillips received £400 and was made a groom of the King's bedchamber and Chancellor of the Duchy of Lancaster. They had laboured hard and risked all, while Jones had merely stabled the royal steed, an act that would have been treated as treasonous by the Parliament and in normal circumstances might have been expected to reap some small reward. Since then, despite having set out bravely with Penruddock, he had definitely blotted his copybook in the Crown's eyes.

By what possible means could Francis Jones have avoided execution for the Penruddock affair? The answer was clear in the minds of his contemporaries who, as Dove's fulminations show, knew full well that he was related to Oliver Cromwell. It can have done his reputation no good among Royalists. Even so he was lucky that the compromising letters he had written stayed walled up in an attic of Secretary Thurloe's London house until workmen came across them in the eighteenth century. But Francis did not escape all punishment. Whereas he kept his head on his shoulders, keeping his property was another matter.

In that respect he lost heavily. He was almost certainly pressed to sell his estate to one of Cromwell's cronies and did not recover it at the Restoration. The restored king was unwilling to upset too many of the senior Puritans by obliging them to return Royalist land they had acquired during Parliamentary rule. Charles went out of his way to ratify the Roundhead acquisitions. Francis proved in no position to buck that trend.

Oddly, Oliver Cromwell's eighteenth-century biographer, Rev. Mark Noble, a man close enough to the times to have known descendants of the Cromwells still in possession of family memorabilia, wrote that 'it is singular, that we know of none of the protectoress' relations that interested themselves during the civil wars...' He was wrong about Francis and his brother John, whose grandmother, having being born a Crane, was in her own right aunt to the so-called 'Protectoress', Cromwell's wife, and furthermore had married Oliver's uncle after her Jones husband had died. This double relationship, which might not seem especially close in modern eyes, was enough to save the brothers from execution or transportation. At that genealogical distance Cromwell himself had a wide kinship and was related to many members of parliament, while as we noted Penruddock drew heavily on his own kin for recruits to the Rising. Such links were indispensable at a period when nepotism reigned. What follows in this chapter gives a little of the flavour, but only a little, of the detective work involved in following the misty leads about the Wiltshire Joneses and the connections, fortunate and unfortunate, that linked them to Cromwell. We must not stand shivering on the edge of the genealogical pool, sketching history only as silhouettes. To reach the realities of the period we must plunge into its murky depths.

Jones is not a name to conjure with and deciding which individual Jones the sources may mean is undeniably arduous. Out of fashion though it is, or at any rate kept at a remove from the mainstream, genealogy has to be considered in order to grasp the full events of history. The fact that the following account is substantially regional may also bemuse at first with its array of Wiltshire place names but concentrating on one area helps the analysis by restricting the diffuseness found in national histories, where unrelated examples from hither and yon are clumped together. Initially concentrating on Wiltshire makes sense, not only because of the Penruddock connection and the county's general prominence in national affairs in the seventeenth century (Clarendon, chronicler of the Civil War, came from there) but because it was copiously

described by an antiquary of lasting importance: John Aubrey. Sidelights
on the property market and personal conflicts of the time appear in local
and regional studies, bringing the period into bolder relief. For all that,
using the microscope of local research does not always make things as
clear as might be hoped. E. G. H. Kempson, a Marlborough antiquary,
compiled a family tree of the Joneses from parish registers and two
further sources, the Visitation of Wiltshire of 1623 which lists descents of
the gentry and the *Inquisitiones post mortem* of 1632. He twice appended
to his manuscript a note to the effect that the *Inquisitiones* make 'some
ambiguous statements re youngest generation.' The ambiguity is never
fully resolved and the tale never finally made complete.

Even so Francis Jones's family background does help towards
solving the puzzles concerning him: who he was, how he became the
third man among the principals in the Penruddock conspiracy but the
only one to escape beheading, and why he sold his estate at Newton Tony,
Wiltshire, the following year. The fate of his brother John, likewise of
Newton Tony, is more obscure. John had been admitted to the Middle
Temple in 1647, became Captain John Jones during the civil war and was
arrested along with Francis when Penruddock failed. Much later Captain
John returned to die at the old family home of Woodlands, Minal, and
in 1670 left a will. No documents explain John's possibly ignominious
return. He left no land although he did make bequests to servants. By
1670 the Wiltshire land held by the Jones family as a whole had been
gradually sold off whereas fifty years earlier there had been six manors.

Of all the memorials I have sought, the most frustrating is the
joint plaque at Minal to the ancestors of Francis and John, William and
John Jones, father and son, who died in 1610 and 1611. The original
Wiltshire Joneses had arrived in the 1530s from a country house in
Wales. Their story parallels that of another Anglo-Welsh family, the
Williamses. Both had Norman blood and long Welsh genealogies dating
from when the younger sons of Normans originating around Gloucester
were invading the Vale of Glamorgan. Medieval descendants married
Welsh women and adopted the Welsh system of naming, although the
surname Jones is by no means exclusively Welsh, being essentially
Johnson and commemorating Saint John. The Williamses and Joneses
made marriages within their own circles in both Wales and England
– 'the sort of arrangement, complicated to describe, which was often
found convenient at that time for considerations of property as well as
propinquity.' This is a quotation from Antonia Fraser, who caught the

essence neatly when writing about the Williams family. She understood, as Rev. Noble did not, the legal significance of Welsh genealogies.

The difference between the Williamses and the Joneses was that the former adopted the name Cromwell in gratitude to a rich relative. Oliver Cromwell himself also had a royalist uncle and, so Wagner says in *Pedigree and Progress,* was linked by a lateral chain of only three families to a family of Lauds, probably that of the arch-Anglican Archbishop Laud himself. Furthermore the marriage of Cromwell's son in 1665 was to link his line to the Stuarts with only two intervening families. In the seventeenth century the Williamses aka Cromwells entered the Joneses family story too but the Joneses went on calling themselves plain Jones. Their fortune had been made by one of their own number and name, William Jones of Woodlands, Minal, a late Tudor land speculator who is named on the joint Minal plaque.

William Jones had built up a property portfolio by taking an active part in the land transactions of the expansionary Elizabethan age. Through farming the property called Minal Woodlands which they rented from the Hungerfords, preeminent Wiltshire landowners who owned eighty-five manors and vast sheep flocks, the Joneses made sufficient money to set about buying land on their own behalf. They also ran the large Woodlands warren where the rent was levied in couples of rabbits. Accounts of their husbandry are published in the Wiltshire Record Society series. William Jones was rich enough to be among those who 'lent' James I £16.13s.4d in the second year of his reign and was able to extend his interest to other manors, relying on patronage, as was usual in early modern times.

William Jones was not averse to lending money if the security was good, as it seemed to be in the case of Fyfield Manor, Wiltshire. It lay next door to a property he had built up in the parish of Milton Lilbourne, where he owned the advowson (the right to select the clergyman). Fyfield had descended since 1200 in a family called Warin or Warren. In 1595 William Warin took the opportunity of borrowing £300 from Jones on the security of the manor, then worth £20 per annum but defaulted and in 1598 Jones brought an action against him at Marlborough. He did not appear in court and could not be found. The Sheriff was directed to capture the runaway, if 'it is sufficiently attested, that the aforementioned [William Warin] lurks and runs about in your county.' Whether the debt was eventually repaid is not recorded but Fyfield was one manor the Joneses never obtained.

Among the half-dozen manors that William Jones did succeed in acquiring the most ambitious was his purchase in 1584 of Stratton St. Margaret, including Over Stratton, Nether Stratton and somewhere called the Thorpe. Stratton St Margaret was a tiny place outside Swindon long since swallowed up by the town. Stratton lay between Swindon and Highworth, then small hilltop market towns of which Swindon became the greater only during the Civil War. Highworth was besieged, its market lost pre-eminence and its rival developed an additional advantage through quarrying a white stone suitable for paving the interiors of houses. Strictly speaking, Jones took only a lease on the Stratton land but since this was to run for 2,000 years the transaction amounted to a purchase in anyone's book. With no false modesty, he proposed converting the manor into 'Stratton Jones', not that the idea was wholly original among holders of the name of Jones – one of the manors in Ashford Carbonell, Shropshire, was called 'Ashford Jones' from the fourteenth century until at least 1807.

In the Wiltshire Local Studies Library is a typescript, 'Account of the Manor of Stratton St. Margaret' by E. C. Elwell, the longer title of which describes it 'as taken from Deeds and Papers in this Box' by Edward Charles Elwell, 1928. Elwell was a Highworth solicitor whose firm held documents that had come down through the Goddards, long the leading Swindon family. Seventy-five years after Elwell put pen to paper the notation 'in this Box' was no longer an obvious help. Which box? Luckily someone had inserted a Wiltshire Record Office Accession number and the documents that Elwell used can be found in the Archives. Most relate to leases taken up or relinquished by the Joneses and are not otherwise informative.

Elwell's own account invited study. He might have been engaging in detective work purely out of interest but he was a solicitor at heart and concentrated on the descent of the Stratton manors, an exercise that would nowadays be spurned as antiquarianism. No doubt this sort of investigation could be make-work for lawyers but complex titles do tend to raise doubts and country solicitors assure me that very old deeds may still need to be examined, just as to this very day eighteenth-century enclosure awards are occasionally drawn on in boundary disputes. The anomalies and obscurities are hard to explain to modern economic historians, who wish (and therefore believe) the categories in the records to be cut-and-dried. Elwell became exasperated because he could not locate on the ground where the various Stratton manors had been. A capital tenement in Stratton Jones was mentioned but he could not identify its site. What the documents in question reveal was how long after all connection with the Joneses had been severed that their ownership was still being cited. The Joneses sold out in 1625 but Elwell noted that as late as 1751, 'Mr Goddard claims Jones' Manor at Stratton. (The Manor appears to be described in some of the documents in various names amongst other (sic) Stratton Jones...' It was indeed so called in a number of seventeenth- and eighteenth century documents. Goddard's claim was lodged against a Mr. Blandy, who in 1751 insisted he was the person 'seized and possessed' of the Manors of Stratton St. Margaret and Stratton Jones. The very same day a Swindon solicitor shot back to Goddard that there was no need for dismay, 'Jones Manor may probably be divided he part and you part.'

The interest here relates to the long hangover of the Stratton Jones name. This is a central point with respect to the efficiency, or rather inefficiency, of institutions. Had ownership been easy to state unambiguously there would have been no need for reference to earlier descents. As it was, disputes were all too likely and cumbersome methods were needed to demarcate properties. English leases went on specifying the bounds of farms not in terms of measured surveys but by transient features like trees. In 1699 the agriculturist, John Worlidge, speaking of big old timber, asked rhetorically, 'what can be more pleasant than to have the bounds and limits of your own property preserved and continued from age to age by the testimony of such living and growing witnesses?' Even in Acts of Parliament the citing of trees continued until at least the 1830s. Field Maple is said to have been favoured because it is slow growing. But trees are not immortal and no certainty could arise from treating them as if they were. Even the modern Land Registry makes it clear that plans for a property show only 'general boundaries' and cannot be relied on for establishing in feet and inches exactly where they run. Accordingly a majority of property disputes are over boundaries, which was true *a fortiori* in the past. The landed classes doubtless put up with the fees demanded by lawyers for making sense of the inconsistent documents that resulted because proper certification was valuable and because high fees had the latent function of restricting the number of people who could afford to mount challenges in the courts.

Early in the seventeenth century the Joneses had begun to lease out and sell off their Stratton land. The Milton Lilbourne properties were disposed of in stages during the 1620s and one of the several

family members confusingly called John Jones sold the remainder in
1640. Apart from some parcels of land they held in Minal, the manor of
Rockley was owned the longest. In the middle of the seventeenth century
it remained in the hands of William Jones's great-grandson, John, but
not for much longer. The expansion of late Tudor times was over and a
progressive, or rather regressive, disposal of assets was under way.

The family seems to have been affected by a major set-back right
at the start of the seventeenth century, perhaps commercial but more
likely political or religious. The deaths of William Jones and his son
followed in close and unexpected succession but there was more to the
trouble than that, as came to mind on reading James Waylen's *History of
Marlborough,* published in 1854. Waylen's sympathies were not with the
Cavaliers, who had set fire to his town. He had obtained access to the
municipal documents only after agreeing to temper his interpretation
of this phase of the Borough's history. Speaking of Minal, which is hard
by Marlborough, he condescended to cite John Aubrey in admitting that
the glass in the church had been spoiled by the Cromwellians in the
'late warres.' Waylen drew from Aubrey the further information that
Minal church contained an inscription to William Jones, dated 1610.
This rubric was in the south aisle and was the only inscription in the
church, though there was an escutcheon of the Marquis of Hertford,
who was a Royalist general, and the arms of the Hungerfords, who
were also Royalists. Aubrey had made his visit in 1660, establishing
that the plaque survived at that time. 'Come all to justice', began the
inscription in Latin, continuing in English, 'Here lyeth the body of
William Jones, Gentilman, who departed this life the 8th of Nov. 1610...
And here sleepeth with his father the body of John Jones, Gent., his
son, whose dayes also ended shortly after, being the 28th of January the
same yeare' – that is 1610 by the old calendar but 1611 in modern terms.
The usual praise for the father's honesty, charity and Christian faith is
included, 'deservedly commended by the Preacher at his funeral.' The
key phrase is the final one, which states that the two Joneses '...received
their salvation whilst the world doth persecute them.'

Minal church is full of ornamentation. John Betjeman thought it
the perfect Georgian church: 'you walk in to the church of a Jane Austen
novel, into a forest of magnificent oak joinery.' This was provided on
the initiative of the Rector of 1816, who had found the church, 'deeply
in decay'. He persuaded twelve of his better-off parishioners to hire a
master carpenter to design and build shoulder-high pews and put up

wall panelling, a gallery and other woodwork. Each farm in the parish had its own box pew. The Jones's plaque was covered up by the panelling, not to see the light of day again until restoration work in 1981.

Among the notes of the antiquary, Kempson, is a scrappy, undated draft letter intended to be sent by two or three people, identified only by their initials, to Captain Stanning of Mildenhall House. He may have been chairman of the Parochial Church Council. The letter states that the senders 'are very interested to know that the memorial to William and John Jones was rediscovered behind the panelling on the east wall of the south aisle. As well as being an early memorial (1610) it is also of historical interest... May we express the hope that this memorial will not be entirely hidden again when the panelling is replaced. I understand that your architect can suggest a way in which this can be done.' The letter must have been drafted in 1981 or 1982, when dry-rot in the woodwork and decay of the stone meant that the wood had to be replaced by new oak, the carvings re-made and a general restoration undertaken. It was in the course of this work that the plaque was rediscovered. Nevertheless, in the early twenty-first century it is once more completely unclear where the inscription might have been. Obviously the authorities had not acted on the request in the letter, if ever they received it, and a local historian reports that the inscription was covered again by the new panelling.

What did the inscription imply? It is curious because the plaque was dated a generation after the deaths of William and John Jones in 1610 and 1611:

WI LL

16 42

Do the letters add up to the name Will as in William Jones or are they two sets of initials. If so, whose is the latter pair? WI might be William Jones, since I could stand for J at that date, but LL rings no bells. Inscriptions were usually written by the incumbent, which may be significant because until he was ejected by the Parliament the living of Minal was held by George Morley, a convinced Royalist. After leaving his parish in 1648 Morley accompanied a friend to the scaffold where the man was executed for Royalist plotting. Immediately afterwards Morley left to join Charles II on the continent. He became royal chaplain at Breda when Charles was waiting in exile. Although in turn his Parliamentary replacement was ejected from Minal in 1660, Morley did not come back but went on to become, first, Bishop of Worcester (a rich port town on the Severn), then Bishop of Winchester. He was also a friend of Izaac Walton, author of *The Compleat Angler*, which speaks in his favour. It seems likely that Morley or his supporters in the parish devised a belated memorial to the two Joneses in order to make a politico-religious statement. If William and John Jones were as Royalist as seemingly they were, they lived too close to Puritan Marlborough to have dodged what the plaque refers to as earthly persecution.

The Mallet Arms, Newton Tony, on the site of the Jones' and Fiennes' manor house.

From these enigmas we turn to the legacy as far as it concerned Francis and John Jones and Newton Tony. During the 1590s, William Jones had bought the manor of Newton Tony. This was the purchase that led ultimately to his descendants' dangerous involvement with John Penruddock and their narrow avoidance of the fate of Penruddock and Hugh Grove. Execution was averted but in 1656, the year after the Rising, Francis Jones sold Newton Tony manor to the arch-Puritan Nathaniel Fiennes, second son of Lord Saye and Sele, whose daughter Celia was born there. Celia's famous book of travels repeatedly mentions starting and finishing her journeys at Newton Tony but never describes the parish. The most she says is that it 'is all on the downs in fine Champion [open] Country pleasant for all sport, Rideing, Hunting, Courseing, Setting and shooting.' The attraction to sporting gentry was plain.

The histories of Newton Tony manor and of the Joneses are thoroughly entwined but it is useful to try to unravel them to reveal the complications surrounding marriage, property and politics in gentry society. A few dense paragraphs are unavoidable to work through the tangle of relationships; even then the disentangling can be managed only up to a point, because the sources are as gappy as the hawthorn hedges that run across the chalk downs. As a curate wrote in the parish registers of Aldbourne, Wiltshire, 'no records kept in the time of civil disorder' and the same might be said of many another parish. As to the extra difficulty of tracing the Joneses, there were at least four Captain John Joneses on one side or the other during the Civil Wars, three of them proving not to be Captain John Jones of Newton Tony! Further confusion sometimes arises with Colonel John Jones, a brother-in-law of Oliver Cromwell who was hanged, drawn and quartered as a regicide at the Restoration.

Newton Tony manor had been bought in 1581 by Thomas Crane, who was of Upwood, Dorset, but significantly was a member of an East Anglian family. The oddity is that when William Jones acquired the property in turn in 1599 he did so on behalf of one of Crane's four daughters, the youngest, who was due to marry his own grandson, John Jones, in 1603. In 1599 she was merely twelve or thirteen. Presumably she had been betrothed to John as a child and her future father-in-law was marking the event by buying the manor in her name. Her Christian name, Eluzai, was unique, appearing only once in the Bible. When her father died in 1596 her sisters are stated as being 17, 18 and 19 without any months and days stipulated yet she was recorded as only nine years, eleven months and twenty days old. Special importance must have attached to the extreme precision with which Eluzai's age was stated.

When John Jones married Eluzai he was stepping into a hornet's nest. It appears that his grandfather had not bought Newton Tony manor directly from Eluzai's father but from the husband of one of her sisters. He was a David Waterhouse. In November 1605, John Jones and two of his three brothers-in-law, the husbands of three of the four Crane sisters, felt obliged to bring an action before the Star Chamber alleging forgery of Thomas Crane's will. The action, in which they prevailed, was aimed at the fourth brother-in-law, Waterhouse, who was an able man but sounds a bit like Mr. Toad.

Crane family connections ran back, crossed Royalist and Roundhead lines, and spread outwards in several directions; for example, as early as 1592 two Penruddocks were named in an indenture concerning all four of Thomas Crane's daughters. Thomas Crane himself was related to the Groves, the family from which came Hugh

Grove, the other leading Penruddock rebel. As if these cross-connections were not bewildering enough, we now come to the crux of the family relationships which explain the outcome for Francis and John Jones. Their grandfather, the John Jones who was Eluzai's husband, died in 1611. But in 1614 she married again, this time Henry Cromwell of Hinchinbroke, Huntingtonshire, who as late as 1617 was still using as an alias (in the sense of an alternative) the old Welsh name of his family, Williams. Henry was Oliver Cromwell's uncle. Eluzai's second marriage was the key to the escape of her grandsons from execution or transportation after the Rising.

Despite owning Upwood, Dorset, the Cranes were really Suffolk people, which is possibly how Henry and Eluzai had met. Oliver Cromwell and his wife, Elizabeth Bourchier, were both related to the Cranes. Oliver's wife was Thomas Crane's granddaughter and Eluzai, as one of Crane's daughters, was therefore her aunt, hence Oliver became Eluzai's nephew by marriage! How Oliver really did meet his wife is a matter of conjecture. The Cromwell Association guesses it was because his wife's aunt had married his uncle, though it occludes the Jones connection by describing her as Eluzai Crane - she had not been a Crane since before she married for the first time and was correctly the widow, Eluzai Jones. This is where the general lack of scholarly scruple concerning the name Jones starts to appear, befuddling the genealogical and historical record. Even when the Jones attribution is correct, other mistakes occur, as when the Biographical Register of St John's College, Cambridge, states that Henry Cromwell married Eliza [sic], daughter of Thomas Crane of Newton Tony and – dismissively - the widow of 'one Jones'.

The eldest son of John and Eluzai Jones was a Francis, who married Ann Ryves (pronounced Reeves) of Ranston, Dorset, on 6th June, 1625. Their wedding was at Iwerne Courtney, a place alternatively called Shroton (to add to England's endemic topographical confusion both names are still in use today). The marriage forged interesting links with a further set of relatives and politically relevant connections. There were two lines of Ryves, one at Damory Court, Blandford, and Ann's, the junior branch, nearby at Ranston. The Ryves family had acquired extensive lands in Tudor Dorset and were 'numerous, healthy and gifted in the seventeenth century.' In 1684 references were made to 'the Worthily Honored George Ryves of Ranston Esq' and 'a flourishing Branch of that fairly spreading and diffusive Family of the Ryves.'

Arms of the Ryves family
of Damory Court, Blandford
and of Ranston House,
Iwerne Courtney

*left: Translation of the epitaph of Ann Ryves (died 1652) at Newton Tony, Wiltshire.
She was the mother of Francis and John Jones.*
right: Crest of the Ryves family of Blandford and Iwerne Courtney, Dorset

They were strong Royalists and spun off a Virginian branch which has produced a substantial family history and even in the early twenty-first century still visits Dorset.

Although penalised by the Cromwellians in 1645, the Ryves survived the ravages of war at Ranston, which is now hidden from the vulgar gaze by a high wall of the type behind which landowners like to hide. In the Blandford line, George Ryves of Damary Court had a daughter, Katherine, who was John Aubrey's fiancée and his most promising love. But she died in 1657, leaving £350 to him, besides a mourning ring to his mother. Aubrey had been at school at Blandford, as had John Penruddock, and like several of the Ryves men, and indeed the Joneses, he was trained at the Middle Temple. He stayed friends for life with one of Katherine's aunts and we know he was acquainted with the Joneses.

Francis Jones's children were accordingly brought up by a mother who, as a Ryves, came from 'an old and distinguished family' steeped in a strongly Royalist culture. Her brothers had fought as cavaliers and the eldest, George, had been fined heavily. Today the plaque to Ann in

Newton Tony church has been re-set because it was in poor condition and likely to fall off the wall. Its cryptic Latin is translated on a neighbouring notice, which is helpful because the Wiltshire Record Society's volume of Memorial Inscriptions omits the line stating the year in which she died. Ann died at fifty in 1652, leaving three sons and three daughters, two of the sons being the Francis and John who took part in the Penruddock Rising.

Francis and John both owned land at Newton Tony. Both signed the Protestation Returns for the parish in 1641-1642. This was an oath of loyalty to Charles I and was obligatory in theory for all males of over 18 years but it may be significant that the Joneses headed the parish list. The administrator of the Protestation Returns for the whole Salisbury division was John Penruddock. Although Cromwell decried the rebels as of mean condition he was fully aware that the Joneses were his kinsmen and he cannot have meant what he said. An account of the trial acknowledges 'Penruddock, Hugh Grove, Jones, and other persons of condition' and the judge who condemned the rebels admitted they were well educated, meaning the leaders, and cleverer than he was.

The costs of going to war and subsequent Parliamentary fines had already made their loyalty to the Crown expensive. John Jones's resources may have been depleted by the exactions proposed in 1649 by an Edward Curtt, who comes across as a bounty hunter. A letter from him was read to the Committee for Advance Money coupling John with the much richer Lawrence Washington of Garsdon as targets for squeezing. Curtt's letter reads, 'That Captain Jones, of Newton Tony, in the County of Wilt., was in Armes agt. the Parliament, his estate about 400// per anm., as I am informed.' There is no record of the fine being collected but the possibility remains that Curtt had to be bought off. That may be what happened since no identifiable Jones of Newton Tony appears in the list of Wiltshire compounders, although a Jo. Jones does figure in the general rolls for the county. The Washingtons continued in possession of Garsdon and had prominent descendants. In view of the Royalist nature of that colony it is no surprise that a later member of the family, George Washington, was a Virginian.

The Washingtons were much closer neighbours to the Joneses than is suggested by the location of Garsdon, which is in north Wiltshire, because they also possessed land in south Wiltshire only half-a-dozen miles from Newton Tony. Sir Lawrence Washington had bought West Amesbury manor in 1628 and the Washingtons thereafter owned

Stonehenge for over fifty years. The aim of the purchase had been to acquire what is described in American sources as a 'Hound Dog Kennel'! The sources do not specify but the kennels were either for foxhounds or long dogs for hare coursing. Was using Stonehenge for dog kennels any worse than the aim of Hugh Peters, Fairfax's chaplain and a great favourite of Cromwell, who wanted to pull it down as a pagan temple?

After the war John Jones returned to improve his Newton Tony estate, went away during the Rising and came back again. Aubrey recorded this in his *Natural History of Wiltshire*, compiled between 1656 and 1691. He wrote that, 'Mr Toogood, of Harcot [Hillcot near Pewsey], has fenced his grounds with crab-tree hedges, which are so thick that no boare can get through them. Captain Jones, of Newton Tony, did the like on his downes. Their method is thus: they first runne a furrow with the plough, and then they sow the cakes of the crabbes, which they get at the verjuice mill. It grows very well, and on many of them they doe graffe.' I suspect that 'graffe' means graft.

After Eluzai died, three-quarters of Newton Tony manor descended to the Francis Jones who was her son, though he sold the advowson in 1636. The estate remained in the possession of the Joneses until 1656, the year when Francis sold out. (His nephew continued to own property at Newton Tony but sold this in lots in 1658, 1660 and 1662). Francis's disposal of the manor was not a routine disposal, as if by someone short of cash or moving elsewhere, but was a sale to one of Cromwell's closest associates. Forced sales were an obvious means of punishment for rebellion. Other gentry suffered heavily as a result of being far less involved with Penruddock than the Joneses had been, for instance John Deane of Oxenwood, fifteen miles away, was put to a truly immense amount of trouble. Thomas Mompesson lost out because Cromwell gave Unton Croke £200 per annum out of Mompesson's estate as a reward for defeating Penruddock at South Molton, and made Croke's father a sergeant-at-law. It was a personalised age, not understandable solely in terms of impersonal institutions or generalisations.

According to some accounts, Nathaniel's father, William Fiennes, Lord Saye and Sele, bought Newton Tony for him or he got it through his wife, the extremely religious daughter of the Puritan Colonel Whitehead of Tytherley. Unfortunately no enlightening documents are in the archives or are held by the present Lord Saye and Sele. Either way, Nathaniel Fiennes settled in the village, where his wife ran a conventicle that continued after the Restoration. Even more compromising, her

chaplain, John Crofts, had formerly been chaplain to Alice Lisle, wife of
the regicide who was gunned down in Lausanne.

After the sale of the manor to Nathaniel Fiennes, the Newton Tony
branch of the Joneses starts to descend into obscurity. Tracing them is
easier for two or three in the female line than in the male. Whereas the
males seem to disappear, the women were not wholly cast into the outer
darkness as a result of the connection with Cromwell. One sister of
Francis and John was an Anne who married William Norborne, gent., of
Chute, Wiltshire. Her husband was presumably related to the Royalist,
Walter Norborne of Calne, whose funeral in that weaving town in 1659
was disrupted by the mob. She died aged 47 in November 1681 but her
memorial in Chute Forest, although recorded in *Monumental Inscriptions
of Wiltshire*, did not survive a nineteenth-century church rebuilding. Her
sons did at least matriculate at Magdalen and New College, Oxford, in
the third quarter of the seventeenth century.

In the next generation, Annetta, daughter of the Penruddock
culprit, Francis Jones, married Roger Cooper, son of John Cooper of
far-off Thurgarton, Nottinghamshire. John was involved in an abortive
rising there timed to coincide with the Penruddock Rising but after the
Restoration was appointed Carver to Charles II, as well as tax gatherer
for Nottinghamshire. Carver was an honorary or symbolic appointment
whereas tax-gathering offered personal gain. John's own father was
Sir Roger Cooper who had stoutly defended his manor at Thurgarton
against Col. Hutchinson, governor of Nottingham Castle. Moreover
Francis Jones's own widow, Cecilia, was appointed Rocker to Queen
Anne, another largely honorific post. She superintended the rocking of
the cradles of those doomed infants whom Anne bore before ascending
the throne. Cecilia died in 1693 and was buried in Westminster Abbey.
Her affairs were managed by her daughter, Anne, but from that point
the trail is lost.

How should we evaluate experiences like these? Declining families
are seldom much studied, though a family called the Dodingtons
of Woodlands, Mere, offers something of a parallel. Its fate has been
described on a South Wilts website by a descendant, Mark Wareham,
in an article called 'The Dodingtons of Mere – a "ruined" family.' The
Dodingtons suffered heavy fines and ultimately had to sell their manor
in 1672.

Given land's central importance as a source of wealth and status, it
was a serious, almost mortal, blow for a man to be obliged to relinquish

his estate in the way both Dodington and Jones were. Genealogies are usually judged unsuccessful if the senior male line dies out and the offspring of other sons begin to tumble down the social scale. But that is a one-sidedly masculine view of history. Whatever happened to the sons, genes and culture will have been carried forward by any daughter who made an advantageous marriage. The problem for the historian is that women tend to disappear behind the screen of their husbands' names and their descendants would be difficult to locate. Admittedly, the Cromwells survived through their daughters; descendants of the female lines are still identifiable today but they are a prominent and closely studied family that is in no way typical. Although the experience of other families casts light on how history played out, in the larger scheme of things the fate of any one of them is perhaps of secondary importance. They could lose caste or rank without impairing the fortunes of the social class to which they belonged. Society was elastic enough to survive the loss of its individual parts. What social decline reveals are the forces acting on the group.

5
SHOCKS, RETRIBUTION AND FUSION

THE SHOCKS OF WAR and regime change are worth discussing for the insights they give into the resilience of the economy and the direction of future happenings. We deal first with the effects on Cavaliers who were caught up in the war and repressed by subsequent Parliamentary regimes or punished for actually rebelling, and come secondly to the experience of leading Roundheads after the Restoration.

In the wake of the Rising, the participants were hunted down and rule by the Major-Generals was imposed on the whole community. This was a chill wind, especially the imposition of the Decimation Tax which was so harsh as to make many Royalists irreconcilable. Nevertheless the full implementation of Puritanical restrictions on public behaviour fairly soon tailed off. The Restoration of 1660 was in turn a blow to the Parliamentarians, although it can be stated at once that retribution was unexpectedly limited and the canniest among them had effectively switched sides in advance. There was certainly a great deal of rough show. On the very day of Charles II's Restoration, an effigy representing the Solemn League and Covenant – the agreement of 1643 between Parliament and the Covenanters to alter the English church on Scottish lines - was burned at Ross-on-Wye, Herefordshire. Yet it was only an effigy that was set on fire and no-one was burned at the stake.

While there were exceptions - not everyone likes their relatives, or their wife's relatives – most families clung together to rescue one another from adversity. Outright declarations of the importance of family are surprisingly rare but for an example we can go back to the end of the sixteenth century when the Wiltshireman, Simon Forman the astrologer, got married. He absolutely exulted in the alliances of his wife's parents with fourteen named 'houses of honour and worship' besides 'divers others'. The glee with which Forman recorded the contacts he had acquired and their force in his world are hard to credit now, when the decisions of impersonal institutions are more readily accepted and many people would be hard put to name their second cousins. For another example, note that Oliver Cromwell's grandfather put the arms of his family and those of others to whom he was allied in the glass of the bow windows at Hinchinbroke House, Cambridgeshire. In the past, personal relationships were especially helpful, even vital, because other ways of assessing trustworthiness were fewer and the courts were expensive and not entirely reliable. Personal connections also explain much behaviour when so many families felt rooted in particular districts, despite Thomas Fuller's oft-quoted reservations about the instability of the skittish lands (read: active land market) close to London.

Victorian antiquaries made the study of family trees and manorial descents tedious and they are nowadays largely ignored by professional scholars. This is surely an over-reaction. Economic historians in particular shun delving into the details of genealogy, let alone the circles of friendship, although readings of past economic life can be mysterious without reference to them. John Aubrey's *Brief Lives* makes this clear, yet despite the perennial interest in his book surprisingly little is nowadays made of the fact. But the people of the period tended to know one another or at any rate know of one another. Aubrey himself had made his first auspicious acquaintance with the stone circle at Avebury in the 'empty days after Christmas 1648' when he was out hunting with Colonel John Penruddock. In 1659 he and Sir George Penruddock made themselves churchwardens of Broad Chalke to rescue the church from dilapidation. The personal is one side of historical interpretation although some background in economics is useful too, since without it another slice of behaviour can seem random or purposeless.

Where the gentry of early Stuart times met or how the influential webs formed by their marriages were spun are seldom certain. More documentation survives from later times. Country house life in the eighteenth- and nineteenth centuries is endlessly discussed with reference to balls, hunts, shooting parties and so forth. But activities like these had ancient origins and rural society resumed its round of leisure events soon after the Restoration. At any period the presence nearby of a regiment and its officers tended to set up a matrimonial bazaar. Riding into the county town for the assizes was another common occasion for partying. Penruddock may have meant his horsemen to enter Salisbury while the assizes were in session because at such a time their arrival would have seemed fairly routine.

The troubles of the seventeenth century provoked one abiding reaction among the warring gentry which will be emphasised in what follows - thereafter they closed ranks. During the late seventeenth- and early eighteenth centuries the one hundred or so great noblemen socially above the level of gentry formed, so Anthony Wagner noted in *Pedigree and Progress*, an oligarchy determined to safeguard its successors, build up its estates and remain pre-eminent politically as well as socially. Throughout history the importance of landowners at this and more modest levels sometimes wavered but recovered in social prestige after every downturn. They succeeded in dominating their tenants until the depression of the late nineteenth century and beyond.

Society had certainly been ruptured by the Civil War, to some effects of which we can now turn. The total costs are hard to compute for various reasons, including fragmentary sources and propagandist assertions, to which may be added the insuperable problem of converting monetary values into modern equivalents, given that the market basket of available goods and services is simply not comparable across so many years. Clearly the cost was high and the English myth that warfare in these islands was eminently less vicious than the horrors of the Thirty Years War on the continent is partly chauvinism. In reality the damage done in England was great. By the end of the warfare there had been several massacres and over 150 towns and 50 to 100 villages damaged or burned down. The figures come from Porter's thorough investigation, *Destruction in the English Civil Wars*, which presents many specific examples. He concludes that one in ten of the inhabitants of provincial cities and towns had their houses destroyed and more than 50,000 people were made homeless, which seems rather few in the circumstances. The spatial distribution of this cataclysmic damage was uneven, cities suffering most, but it is also said that over 200 country houses were ruined.

Brief Lives illustrates the murderousness of the times. All this constituted a heavy blow, although the numerical losses may have had less impact than the uncertainty produced by the turmoil: even so neither loss nor uncertainty were perhaps as lasting as may seem likely at first sight, at least as far as the whole economy was concerned. Viewed from our distance in time, the subsequent recovery was surprisingly vigorous. In rural areas, sleeping dogs were sometimes let lie, which may have been for fear of retaliation. Alternatively it may have been because, if one's neighbours took the opposite side, one still had to live with them.

During the civil wars, urban fires were particularly harmful and in those fearful years resources for rebuilding could be slow to materialise. At Beaminster, Dorset, where in 1644 the thatch had been fired by Royalists reportedly disgruntled at the lack of a local welcome, the town was still little more than a heap of ivy-covered ruins seven years later and Charles II declined to halt there. He stopped at a nearby village instead. Like many little manufacturing towns, Beaminster was Parliamentarian in sympathy but seemed unable to bring about recovery from its own resources. At the time proper instruments to aid recovery were weak. Charitable briefs, which were officially sanctioned letters sent around the country to solicit alms, do not seem to have been fully effective in wartime and the introduction of formal insurance schemes awaited the late seventeenth century.

The absence of effective institutions meant depending on individuals, or as the case may be, picking on them. The Cromwellian response to Beaminster's distress was to find a local Royalist and

Manual fire engine, Shaftesbury, Dorset. Even this simple device post-dates the destructive fires of the seventeenth century.

arbitrarily require him to fund the rebuilding of the town. George Penne, a nearby recusant (Roman Catholic) landowner, was selected for the honour of paying £2,000. He had to sell some land to meet this obligation but in the event did not supply all the cash, sparking a formal complaint from the town's officials. Plainly he equivocated which, in the fraught circumstances of the period, was a dangerous manoeuvre; he might have taken it as a warning that in 1645 a neighbouring landowner's wife, Lady Strode of Parnham, a park adjoining Beaminster, had been run through by a Cromwellian solder's sword as she was trying to defend her property.

When the tables were turned by the Restoration in 1660, Penne petitioned for his money back but Charles II preferred to smooth things over and instead gave him the right to hold a twice-yearly fair. This should have suited everybody – Charles because it cost him nothing, Penne because he got the tolls, and the town of Beaminster because it held onto the money already received while benefiting from fairs that might be expected to increase trade. Penne's own subsequent behaviour, callously trading prisoners taken after Monmouth's Rebellion in 1685, shows how deeply antagonisms might continue to run. Nevertheless, opponents managed to go on living closely side by side and for all practical purposes it was not many years before the grievances faded. Charles II's behaviour was remarkably conciliatory towards almost everyone except the regicides who had actually signed his father's death warrant.

Responsibility for the destruction of Beaminster lay with the Royalists but in the country at large blame usually came to be fixed on the Cromwellians. After all they were the losers and after the Restoration might expect a bad press. In the monarchical centuries that followed, upbraiding the Cromwellians for the ravages of Civil War was irresistible. It became part of folk memory, summed up in the old music hall song about the ruins that Cromwell knocked about a bit, a ditty that everybody recognised until at least the mid-twentieth century. Some examples: at Glympton, Oxfordshire, the church guide states that a flagon stolen by Cromwell's soldiers was recognised in London two centuries later and restored to a glass case in the church. Today, though, the case is dusty and empty; perhaps the contents have been stolen again. At Hesset, Suffolk, the church guide claims that when Cromwell's soldiers arrived the villagers gave them the three keys to the parish chest but not the extra iron bar needed to open it, so that the church kept its medieval treasures (until to the disappointment of visitors they were moved to the British museum). Tales like this abound and tend to smack of retro-propaganda by triumphant Royalists who were happy, say, to erect busts of Cromwell like the one that still exists in Worcester, sporting large pointed ears to symbolise his alleged pact with the Devil. After the Restoration, says Everitt, cavalier legends were spawned 'like mushrooms in the dark.'

What were the effects of the warfare if viewed more dispassionately? Despite deaths and destruction, and some initially severe acts of retribution, it can scarcely be said that the worst consequences lasted unduly long. Seen in another light, there was an opportunity for catch-up growth which was sometimes rapidly seized. People were ready, eager perhaps, to pick up their lives and businesses where they had been interrupted, while the stock of knowledge had outlasted the physical knocks of conflict. Useful knowledge remained in the minds of the populace, available to be brought back into use.

A balanced appraisal of war's effects would need to take into account the income-generating effects of rebuilding. No-one can say for sure what the total bill was or how long full recovery took because direct evidence is so patchy, but the extensive destruction of housing meant a need for replacement accommodation which led to the rapid erection of new dwellings. They were reportedly of low quality which must mean that the average value of the housing stock dipped for a time. Porter considers that towns with specialist industries managed to hold onto them and the sense of it is that trade networks persisted, presumably because many business partners were near at hand and could be easily contacted again. If they had been out of touch, it was for only five years or so. The enemies of any particular regime, Royalist or Roundhead, did not ordinarily cut off their noses to spite their faces and once violence ceased they set to work in order to prosper again. Thus, after the execution of Charles I economic activity resumed quite vigorously. It was helped by the Puritan temper of tradespeople who believed the victory of their side was now secure, and by the de facto acquiescence of the landed gentry, who liked the certainty of the times even though they disliked its complexion. Business similarly resumed quite fast after the Restoration.

The geography of conflict had especially affected routes to major strongholds. The swathes of land along the routes were levied and plundered by both sides, hence the semi-impartial resistance by the

Clubmen. Farming and farm produce were constantly at risk of damage and theft. Much woodland was cut down, opportunistically when local order broke down or alternatively because timber was a bank for its owners to draw on when all else failed. Details of the consequences for farming routines are mostly lacking, though we should note that continuity was probably better than might have been expected because many Royalist estates did find their way back into the hands of their original proprietors. Sequestration was sometimes avoided by a family member stepping forward to buy the land, after which it might well be returned to the first owner. Nevertheless the situation was mixed and the effects of the conflict could drag on: for instance at Bletchingdon, Oxfordshire, a high rate at which tithes were levied was accepted out of fear during the wars but became 'customary' and it was much later before the rate was contested again. Local distortions of this type went largely unrecorded or at any rate comments are rare. As already suggested, the greatest impact may have come less from physical damage than from the uncertainty produced by the Damocles sword of violence that hung over the country. The cost of uncertainty is unknowable without information about prior trends of investment.

The opportunities for catch-up after 1649 are not to be minimised. The likelihood is that the lands of Parliament's supporters were enthusiastically managed after the execution of Charles I, when leading Roundheads felt emboldened to build or rebuild mansions. On Royalist estates sequestration fines might have limited investment and hampered innovation, but traditional practices might have been worked more intensively in attempts to compensate. Contrary to talk at the time, the indications are that Royalist landowners typically accustomed themselves to the relative stability of the Commonwealth. Despite grumbling about social and religious impositions, and despite the presence in their midst of residual bands of Cavaliers plotting rebellion, a majority of the gentry seems to have adapted to the Cromwellian order and returned to the business of farming. The resultant peace and prosperity helped to sap support for Penruddock and other rebels. And in the euphoria after 1660, growth rates may have risen again. Innovations are always said to have arrived with Royalist exiles returning from the Low Countries, which means that the stock of knowledge about husbandry became a little larger than it had been in 1640.

When the conflict had turned in Parliament's favour, provincial Royalists were faced with the choices of voice, quiescence or exit.

They could go on fighting what would rapidly have become guerrilla warfare, threatening the well-being of their families and their hold on the family estates; they could retreat resignedly to the land; or they could opt to go into exile. We have seen in the Penruddock Rising the low odds of successful rebellion, given that this rather sorry episode was one of the few occasions when plotters, or some of them, really did turn out to fight. Most revolts remained hypothetical, being still-born, collapsing in disarray or proving to be easily suppressed. Once warfare ended, the simplest response for most of the Cavaliers was therefore to give in, pay the heavy fines laid on them and, for those who did not have to sell up as a result, retreat to farming their land. They could lick their wounds, hoping for that glorious future when the King might again come into his own, but meanwhile they could carry on ordinary rural business.

To give body to these remarks the fate of individual families may be discussed, starting with some who were directly implicated in Penruddock's Rising. Among the rebels who had to sell up was Richard Goldstone of Amport, which lies over the Hampshire border only a brace of villages from Newton Tony. He is listed in *Alumni Oxonienses* as 'Richard Goldstone s of Thomas of Alderley Wiltshire gent St Mary Hall matric 4/6/1641 aged 17'. His grandfather or a great-uncle had married a Margaret Ryves who had been baptised at Iwerne Courtney, Dorset, in 1550. Richard was therefore related to Ann Ryves, wife of Francis Jones, and it is not surprising he was drawn into the Rising. In 1649 he had been driven to sell Amport manor because his fine as a Royalist was too much to pay, although since it was only £150, one-sixth of the value of his estate, he cannot have been supremely rich to start with. The ancient family of Paulets bought the manor from him. He was sufficiently aggrieved to join Penruddock and was among the prisoners taken. At the Restoration, the Paulets were not ousted in Goldstone's favour, despite his sufferings for the Royalist cause, and they held Amport manor for centuries. Some of the Goldstone family did continue as lay rectors in their home village of Alderley, Wiltshire, until 1677 and others became stewards for King's College, Cambridge, in Monxton, a Hampshire parish right next to Amport. The Goldstones had not sunk wholly without trace but they were now mere functionaries at the estate stewards' level rather than landowners in their own right.

Richard Goldstone and others who rode with Penruddock had hazarded their all, but most of the Royalist gentry were all talk and little do, and when they did get as far as starting to rise against Cromwell their moves seldom amounted to much. An example of a still-born revolt was one in Nottinghamshire, far from the Penruddock affair in Wiltshire but utterly unexpectedly connected with the Newton Tony Joneses. The Nottinghamshire affair petered out almost before it started but is worth describing because it reveals once again family relationships of the type on which seventeenth-century life was based.

Prominent in the Nottinghamshire attempt were Cecil and John, sons of Sir Roger Cooper of Thurgarton, who had fought the Roundheads on the spot during the Civil War. His manor of Thurgarton was one of the houses fortified to throw a protective ring around Newark and face off the Parliamentary garrison in Nottingham. The *Memoirs* of Lucy Hutchinson, wife of Colonel John Hutchinson, governor of Nottingham, together with the excellent Thurgarton village history website, provide the details. The key incident came when Thurgarton was attacked in late 1644: one of the musketeers with whom Sir Roger had lined his hedgerows shot and killed a Roundhead officer. As a result, the house was assaulted, captured and plundered, and Sir Roger, his brother, and forty men were sent prisoner to Nottingham, where Hutchinson was their jailer. Freed late in 1646, Sir Roger spent his time in London trying to regain his estate but still had to sell land to pay the fines levied on him.

After a second fight in 1648, Sir Roger's sons, Cecil and John Cooper, were taken prisoner but later freed. They did not give up but became ringleaders in an intended revolt in Nottinghamshire in March, 1655, at the same moment as the Penruddock Rising. The brothers assembled a small force at Thurgarton, filled a cart with weapons and set out towards Sherwood Forest. Only two or three miles along the road three hundred men met at a public house. But on being told they had been betrayed, which presumably meant only that they had lost the element of surprise, some of the men threw their arms into a pond and scattered in the dark. The Cooper brothers were arrested. Cecil was permitted to leave the country and John escaped, probably to the Low Countries.

John's son Roger married Annetta, daughter of Francis Jones of distant Newton Tony. A connection between the Wiltshire Joneses and the Nottinghamshire Coopers may seem surprising but marriages at a distance were not unheard of, as is rather ironically confirmed by the marriage of their foe, Colonel Hutchinson. Although of Owthorpe, Nottinghamshire, Hutchinson had married Lucy, daughter of Sir John

St. John of Lydiard Tregoze, Wiltshire. Lucy's *Memoirs* say that the north of England had such 'a formidable name among the London ladies' that her husband permitted her to live ten miles out of the city for a while to wean her off London, where she had grown up, and thus prepare herself for the plunge into the northern wilds. Whether Annetta Jones was also allowed a foretaste of unfamiliar parts is not known.

That astringent Oxford historian, J. P. Cooper, observed that, 'the proper unit for the study of great landowners is the family, and their interests usually crossed county boundaries. It is only misguided county archivists and local historians of today who too often attempt by Procrustian treatment of family archives to confine them within such boundaries.' Kinship spilled over the borders of counties, which is what the present saga confirms. Penruddock's followers were related to him or were his neighbours or connections of a sort. They lived in Wiltshire or counties contiguous to it and the link with Nottinghamshire was virtually happenstance. Co-ordinating a plot and uprising on a national level – though it was projected – was extraordinarily difficult and reasons of prudence tended to keep plots within regional bounds. The most that Royalist plotters could hope for was that local risings against Cromwell would erupt simultaneously and merge later, not that they would start out centrally organised or controlled.

At the Restoration the Cooper brothers came home and in December, 1660, Captain Cecil Cooper vengefully ordered the private house of Col. Hutchinson to be plundered. In later life, Cecil, who became Deputy Lieutenant of Nottinghamshire, did make some amends but the first flush of victory had not lent itself to kindly gestures. John Cooper was appointed 'Carver to his Majesty' – one of the honorific positions which were all Charles II could afford as tokens for his supporters. John was also made tax collector for the county, a potentially lucrative office but in some ways doubtless a poisoned chalice too. Of their father, Sir Roger, who died in 1657, Thoroton, the great historian of Nottinghamshire, wrote that he was 'a worthy honest gentleman whose fidelity and constancy to the royal interest wrecked his fortune.' Thoroton added that Cecil would face a hard task repairing the family house and estate, although it was the case that Cecil was buried in Thurgarton church under a marble slab, which was scarcely the mark of a pauper.

The Cooper brothers' exiles had been voluntary or semi-voluntary. Exile typically meant retreating to the European continent and continuing the war there in the guise of day-dreaming, hanging on the words of agents lately arrived from England, and joining court factions. Once Charles I had been executed, the exiles felt they were attending his son's foreign court as the court of the *de jure* king of England. Some chose to do so and go on politicking, as it were, in the air. In their suspended state they were like samurai, swords for hire. Only the most adventurous among them chose distant action over ethereal hope. One of the most active was Marmaduke Langdale, commander of the Northern Horse which had scourged Salisbury. He went into exile in Paris in 1646 and after returning to further defeat in the Second Civil War was banished from England in perpetuity. (Interestingly, he had twice escaped from Nottingham Castle). In 1652 Langdale entered the service of Venice and fought against the Turks but was back in Brussels by 1655. There he sat, resentful at his exclusion from plans for the risings of that year but involved closely enough to complain that he was the one who was obliged to cope with wearisome negotiations about Leveller involvement. Langdale's travels were exceptional and for him the cost of war was great. He had to beg off attending Charles II's coronation because he could not afford to dress himself in the expected style.

Langdale had at least fought long and hard for the Stuarts. Some lesser Royalists were quick to choose avoidance rather than resistance, exit rather than voice. Other destinations for disaffected men throughout the seventeenth century were right outside Europe, even further afield than Langdale's, and proved to be fundamental in shaping the social geography of the Atlantic world. First were the Puritans who had sailed to New England during the early seventeenth century in search of religious freedom. From the start of the 1640s a number of them, including some clerics, sailed back to fight the good fight on Parliament's side. William Hooke, who had emigrated to New England in the 1630s, actually came back to become Oliver Cromwell's chaplain. At Cromwell's behest other returnees went to Ireland, where they were granted land seized from the native Irish and in some instances held it until the twentieth century. New England's Puritan temper was such that at the Restoration it provided a refuge for a handful of Regicides fleeing Charles II's retribution on his father's murderers.

New England would have made an unwelcoming billet for Royalists but there were American colonies friendly to them, the chief being Virginia. It was mainly there that young Cavaliers who had experienced defeat sailed as early as 1647. Virginia closely reproduced the life of southern English landowners. The great houses of eighteenth-century Virginia and Carolina have been described by the American historian, William E. Dodd, as not unlike the 'castles' of a Seymour or Craven in southern or western England. Most of the Virginian elite, as David Hackett Fischer observed in his masterly work *Albion's Seed*, were the sons of strongly Royalist families, were devoutly Anglican, had rural proclivities and manorial ideas, exalted notions of their own honour and paraded the rudiments of an Aristotelian education. Not surprisingly, therefore, one of John Penruddock's brothers, condemned for his part in the Rising, petitioned to be sent to join this community instead of being shipped to Barbados.

In an exceptional and enlightening take on the history of Southern England, Fischer portrays the region in the scarcely distorting mirror of seventeenth-century Virginia. His depiction of Virginian society is valuable for our purposes through indicating what rural England might have been like had the Cavaliers won the second Civil War or been able to overthrow Oliver Cromwell speedily. They did not become dominant until the Restoration, after which Southern England and Virginia did prove remarkably alike. The chief difference was the scale of slavery in the latter, something acceptable to the cavalier mind but not needed, if that is the term, in England. Apart from this, Charles II's desire to obviate any tendency for further revolt placed some slight constraints on Cavalier behaviour at home. A prime example was his unwillingness to eject Parliamentarians wholesale from land they had acquired during the Interregnum.

Much of the social geography of the Atlantic world, which lasted into the nineteenth and twentieth centuries and continues to echo today, originated in dispositions laid down in the Cromwellian era and quickly confirmed under Charles II. The origins are plain enough. What is needed in order to establish that these years were one formative block of time is to explain how the arrangements persisted so long, an elucidation that is of path dependency in which the events of each period lead inexorably to the next. A precise correspondence is not of course to be expected. Too many confounding factors occur in the long run for the outcomes to be identical. In the eighteenth century, Southern England was unable to separate itself from the northern half of the country, where support for Puritan values continued high and the most vigorous industrialisation took place. Virginia, on the other hand, was situated in a larger country with greater differences among its regions

and remained significantly detached from the equivalent industrialising
north, New England. Its cavalier attitudes were (even) less restrained
than those of post-Restoration Southern England. More recently than
Fischer, much more recently than Dodd, and speaking of a wider area
than merely Virginia, another trans-Atlantic historian, James Huston,
says that 'the plantation of the South [was] a fledgling duplicate of the
British estate agricultural system, while the northern family farm came
to be its opposite in nearly every aspect.' This distinction is a staple of
American social history.

To Royalist men (and women) in both England and the Chesapeake
colonies, liberty was strictly hegemonic. Those Americans who dissented
strongly from cavalier values lived at a safe remove in Massachusetts
and had little influence on Virginian life until after the American Civil
War. In England, digesting the defeated Roundheads and deflecting
the energies of irreconcilable non-conformists was bound to suffuse
politics, though a renewal of open conflict was avoided. The English
gentry were helped in their ascendancy because after 1660 they replaced
experienced local officials, who were seen as politically unreliable. The
Tory gentry may have been less efficient but were then able to run local
government free from significant local opposition.

A study of seventeenth-century wealth distribution in Gloucestershire and the Chesapeake colonies of Virginia and Maryland shows the
two areas to have been much alike, with large numbers of poor at the
bottom of society and an elite comprising only 10 to 12 per cent of the
population at the top. They were different societies from, respectively,
Lancashire or Massachusetts. Societies of their complexion flourish best
on a basis of commodity production and exports, wool in Gloucestershire,
tobacco in Virginia, where the rents are fairly easy to cream off and the
demand for high-value labour is weak. (Rents in this respect means the
unearned surplus from mere ownership of the land, not the property rent
of common usage). Crop production and extensive forms of livestock
farming inculcate less skill than manufacturing and help to maintain
hierarchical types of society where the development of a middle class is
limited. Land and the wealth to which farming gave rise were concentrated
in the hands of small elites. Virginia was hyper-Royalist and actually
proclaimed Charles King of England ahead of the Restoration! The
governing Council granted Virginian land lavishly to its own members
and after 1660 a vast tract of two million acres that Charles II bestowed
on his supporters fell into the possession of a single family.

Fischer quotes an historian who compared the genealogies of Virginian families to 'a tangle of fishhooks, so closely interlocked that it is impossible to pick up one without drawing three or four after it' – a striking metaphor that would describe the rural southern English elite too. At the bottom of the social scale, Virginia's lower class was comprised of artisans to only half the extent of New England and was far more rustic. It was much less literate than in Massachusetts. The servant class was 'more highly stratified, more male-dominant, more rural, more agrarian, less highly skilled, and less literate.'

Nor was this an accident. Fischer claims that the royalist elite in Virginia succeeded in manipulating migration to create the type of society they favoured. Like their relatives in Southern England, they were inegalitarian in temper, being prideful gentlemen thinking themselves, and being thought, unapproachably above the common herd. Two centuries later, Southern plantation owners still saw themselves as the descendants of English cavaliers. Jefferson Davis, a slave-owner and the Confederate president during the American Civil War, contrasted them with the lower-class Yankee northerners, although in truth his own paternal grandparents were Welsh rather than descendants of English gentry. Southern states offered an extended array of deferential relationships, so Fischer observes of the white population in Virginia. Black slaves were trapped at the base of this pyramid. Given the elite's preferences it is scarcely astonishing that two centuries after the English Civil Wars the cycle of conflict repeated itself. When the Confederacy lost the American Civil War an estimated 20,000 diehards moved on again, this time to Brazil. Their descendants still live there and still celebrate the Confederacy in the loudest echo of civil war on either side of the Atlantic.

Virginia was the prime destination for Royalist exiles and emigrants, but they also thought Maryland desirable. Aubrey dreamt of going there. The Brookes of Whitchurch, Hampshire, really did go. Theirs was a well-connected family but like many families of rural gentry it had not long since descended from rich London merchants. Moreover, perched in their family tree was a marriage to a daughter of Thomas Dolman, the leading employer of spinners in sixteenth-century Newbury, although country life had diluted or disguised any manufacturing origins by the time Robert Brooke, an Anglican minister, entertained Charles I at Whitchurch in 1644. The king's execution unsettled Brooke and in 1650 he emigrated to Maryland with eight sons, two daughters and twenty-eight servants. He took his flock of sheep and pack of foxhounds with him – reputedly the packs of South Maryland still descend from his hounds, thereby trumpeting the importance of blood sports to both the English gentry and their colonial descendants. One of Brooke's sons went to Harvard and after the Restoration another became a Privy Counsellor. Stay-at-home members of the Brooke family continued however to find life in England difficult and scattered away from Whitchurch, indicating Robert Brooke's sagacity in moving his family across the Atlantic.

Not everyone's beliefs were similarly committed. Turncoats were many, such as Francis Jones and the others 'turned' by Secretary Thurloe, besides those who opportunistically shifted allegiance with little prompting. Edward Montagu, whose family had bought the Cromwell family home in Cambridgeshire, was a Parliamentary colonel in the first Civil war but did not fight in the Second war and in 1660 actually sailed to fetch Charles II back to England. During the wars defectors moved from one side to the other, according to whoever seemed to be winning. Their apostasy shows that for some the normally tight ties of kinship had limits. Not a few of the guilty were executed when caught. Luckier turncoats, cynics or political agnostics included George Monck (above all), Anthony Ashley Cooper and John Wildman.

After the Restoration those regicides who had actually put their signatures to Charles I's death warrant suffered badly. Most of those who failed to skip the country were executed, sometimes horribly. Those who had already died were dug up and their remains desecrated, a barbarity even committed on the bodies of some of their relatives, including Oliver Cromwell's mother and one of his daughters. Afterwards the bodies were thrown into a pit at St. Margaret's, Westminster. Apart from hounding the regicides and other Cromwellians, the greatest persecution – it was more often suppression than actual violence - bore on the non-conformist sects. Membership of the Baptists, Quakers and so forth was taken as code for political as well religious dissent. Yet the larger picture was confused, as is everything connected with the period. Twists and turns abounded, often depending on personal contacts. Given the cross-ties of family bonds and the fact that even during the wars men exchanged private messages with friends on the other side, this was hardly astonishing.

Those Penruddock rebels who escaped execution tended to have their wings clipped but only those who were transported to Barbados suffered desperately. Fines meant that the standard of living of the remainder was reduced, and so by the same token were any resources they might think of using for further rebellion. Cromwell nevertheless ensured that parts of their estates were reserved for the support of their families. The more fortunate, such as Thomas Mompesson from Tidworth, escaped to the continent. He had headed forty horsemen in Penruddock's train but slipped away before the fight and went to France. He and others later filtered home and resumed managing their land.

After the Restoration fines along the lines of Parliament's 'decimation' tax on Royalists were now levied on Roundhead land. Certain estates were confiscated. Once again intervention by powerful kinsfolk might frustrate the edict. Sir Robert Wallop (a regicide but non-signer) owned the manor of Allington, a mere mile or so from Newton Tony. That tiny distance highlights the fact that the Civil War took place in a series of cockpits where people lived cheek by jowl with their opponents. And the fate of Wallop and his property demonstrates, once more, the supreme importance of family connections. Under Charles II his estates were confiscated but his brother-in-law, the Earl of Southampton, interceded on his behalf. The price was letting the Earl acquire Allington, although Wallop's son got back the bulk of the estates.

In person Robert Wallop did not come off well, because in one of the regime's sourer acts of vengeance he was imprisoned for life in the Tower. His wife was permitted to live with him but Wallop was saddled with a chilling memento mori. Every year on the anniversary of the king's execution he was drawn to Tyburn on a hurdle with a halter around his neck. Lord Monson and Sir Henry Mildmay were sentenced to the same fate. In circumstances like these it was important for Roundheads to keep their names off the black list, meaning the list of exemptions from the general pardon that was proclaimed. Wallop did not pull that off. Others succeeded by means of massive bribery. Bulstrode Whitelocke laid out a fortune to ensure that the Commons' vote about exemption went his way. At 174 to 137 the result was scarcely a land-slide in his favour but a miss was as good as a mile when one's head might be on the block.

The fortunes of lesser Roundheads were mixed but are not easy to trace. Even at the time keeping track of former officers and men was often surprisingly difficult. A survey was instituted with varied results, the 1662 list of those in Chepstow comprised only thirty-two men who had borne arms under Cromwell, despite the importance of the place as a jail, whereas assiduous parish constables unearthed fully 1,329 in Staffordshire. Usually royal agents concentrated on those they thought might offer serious opposition, typically former officers.

At first the calls for revenge were strident and were certainly raised in favour of those penalised for their involvement in the Penruddock Rising. The widows of the men executed made an enormous to-do, demanding vengeance on those who had been prominent in the trials. They were led by Penruddock's widow, Arundel, who was by birth a Freke from Iwerne Courtney, the same Dorset parish as Ann (Ryves) Jones. The widows especially attacked the former Lord Chief Justice Rolle, whose presence in court at Penruddock's trial had ironically been meant to create a show of fairness. Yet Rolle's son succeeded in becoming lord of the manor of East Tytherley, became an M.P. for Hampshire and was knighted in 1665. And although the regicide John Lisle was gunned down in Lausanne by vengeful Royalists the Lisle estate at Moyles Court, Ellingham, Hampshire, was returned to his son. All of this must have infuriated Arundel Penruddock. Her revenge was belated, indirect and in the final analysis incomplete. It came about because her son, who was put in charge of searching for fugitives after Monmouth's Rebellion in 1685, tracked down one of them to Moyles Court, where Lisle's widow Alice lived. Judge Jeffreys had Alice beheaded in the market place at Winchester, an act of clemency of a sort, at least compared with being burned alive. Nevertheless the Lisles' daughter survived to marry a future President of Harvard and a great-nephew was the celebrated Hampshire agriculturist, Edward Lisle. Only a novel could do justice to the convolutions.

The body of the regicide, Henry Ireton, was disinterred and maltreated at the Restoration. Supposedly ascetic, he had nevertheless owned a coach and four that cost £200, exposing the hollowness of Puritan restraint. His eldest son, also Henry, acquired the estates of Quenington and Williamstrip, Gloucestershire, through his wife, Catherine Powle. She was the daughter of Henry Powle, a grandson of Oliver Cromwell, who was a landowner and M.P. Along with her husband, Catherine turned Williamstrip into a classical mansion. In that way the Iretons may be said to have had the last laugh.

Estates were confiscated from some leading members of the Parliamentary regime, though not from those Vicars of Bray who had hastened to make peace with the monarch. Whereas Royalist troops had once vandalised Bulstrode Whitelocke's house at Fawley Court, Henley, destroying title deeds and other documents, Whitelocke now presented

Charles with sumptuous volumes from the Royal Library which he disingenuously claimed he had been holding for the King in safe-keeping. The goods of other Parliamentarians were seized, including a large quantity of jewellery from Cromwell's widow. The question arises why the unostentatious Elizabeth Bourchier wanted so much jewellery in the first place, until one realises that royalty always receives presents from the sycophantic whether they desire them or not. And despite her husband's demurral, Elizabeth had for a spell been *de facto* Queen – her two unmarried daughters were usually addressed as Princess by foreign ambassadors and the marriage of one of her daughters was regal, with truly splendid gifts. Oliver himself took to signing documents with the royal 'We'. To complete the see-saw of hypocrisy and chance redolent of the entire period, the husband of one of Cromwell's daughters became an ambassador and privy counsellor under Charles II and was raised to an Earldom by William III. The kaleidoscope of personal fortune laughs at generalisation.

Charles II called a halt to acts of retribution for fear of re-igniting the cycle of revolt. His supporters did not always get their estates back nor recompense for expenses incurred in the Royalist cause. He was more inclined to grant titles which did not cost him actual or immediate cash. Titles were non-pecuniary rewards, some made hereditary and part of the established hierarchy of rank, others merely transient like John Cooper's nomination as 'Carver'. More significant prizes awaited his own illegitimate descendants: as John Wade quipped in *The Black book, or, Corruption unmasked,* there were in the early nineteenth century four dukes, 'in whose veins flow the glorious blood of prostitutes and kings.' A more fundamental part of Charles's legacy was to restore the rotten boroughs, which Cromwell had abolished. Whereas the rise of trade and manufacturing had previously elevated the Commons, under Charles the aristocracy resumed great power.

The king was genuinely grateful to many who had helped him on his escape from Worcester and the descendants of one such family are still in receipt of pensions in the twenty-first century. Some Penruddock rebels also fared well for having taken the risks they did on Charles's behalf. They held on to their estates or regained them and can be found standing for Carolean parliaments. After 1660, Mompesson became M.P. for Wilton, obtained a knighthood in 1662 and acquired the Wiltshire farm of the excise tax for his cousin. Penruddock's own younger son was returned as Member of Parliament for Wilton in 1679.

Robert Mason, a smallish landowner and 'desperate fellow' from near Hereford who had ridden with Penruddock, was knighted. These were rewards for loyalty, a little capriciously bestowed, and reduced in scale by Charles's unwillingness to upset too many people.

After the Restoration it helped that certain leading Parliamentarians had been among the group most willing to bring back Charles II. Monarchical tendencies were already apparent at the top of the Parliamentarian pyramid, among those who thought they might gain by having the ear of only one leader to catch They included John Ashe, the great Wiltshire clothier, the odious Martin Noel, and Nathanial Fiennes. The last named spoke twice in Parliament in favour of crowning Oliver Cromwell. Fiennes's rhetoric urged that, because people found it easier to respect the old names and since the Protectorate was in practice a continuation of monarchical government, why not go the whole hog and restore the title of king? The question was who should that king be? Oliver's son, Richard, was proving indecisive, so despite all that had transpired might not Charles I's son suffice instead?

The point is that there was no Sippenhaft as there was in Nazi Germany and Mao's China, where family mattered even more than in Stuart England and whole families were wiped out for the sins of a single member. No indiscriminate punishments followed 1645, 1649, 1655 or 1660 and it is striking that the sons of opponents were often treated fairly or at any rate not totally stripped of the family property. The legality of their inheritance was accepted, leaving them to continue on the estates from which their errant fathers had been thrust. Despite early acts of vengeance, the ultimate aim of both Parliamentary and Royalist regimes – after 1649 and 1660 respectively - was to tamp down conflict. Charles II in particular felt this was best done by co-opting important figures among his potential opponents. In the short run things cannot have felt benign after the Restoration and undoubtedly people without landed property were discriminated against. Non-commissioned Roundheads and nonconformists clergy who were ejected from their livings in the 1660s cannot be said to have been treated well. Many Roundhead officers or their families, at least the more senior ones, did however receive almost generous treatment. In historical perspective the episodes do tend to bear out the English belief that theirs was a relatively restrained polity.

6

RESTORATION AND SUBLIMATION

URING THE 1650s Charles II sat at The Hague and in other
towns in Western Europe, living on handouts and feeling short of
cash, dickering with the factions who wished to see him restored to his
throne, and spending his ample spare time hawking and womanising.
Exile courts, or at any rate exile households, were also presided over at
The Hague by prominent women, chief among whom was Charles's
aunt, Elizabeth, the Winter Queen. Her husband, Frederick the Elector
Palatine, had lost the Battle of the White Mountain which established
Counter-Reformation and the resurgence of Roman Catholic Europe.
(The aside is irresistible that one soldier in the battle was Descartes).
Frederick afterwards died, leaving Elizabeth in tight circumstances,
although still contriving to keep up a luxurious lifestyle.

The Winter Queen became dependent on the generosity of her
admirer and probable lover, the Earl of Craven, although her modern
biographer, Nadine Akkerman, tells me his subventions were less than
historians typically imply. Nevertheless, Elizabeth was able to hold
court at The Hague and keep up a competition with Amalia Solms,
her former lady-in-waiting who had pulled off the coup of marrying
a Prince of Orange, thereby joining what amounted to royalty in the
United Provinces. The two women vied in extravagant forms of display,
commissioning portraits – they look like sisters in paintings by Gerard
Honthorst – and holding tournaments, ballets and masques. They
bought fashionable clothes, jewellery and every type of rare oddment
from the natural world with which to fill their cabinets of curiosities. As
the somewhat more royal of the two, Elizabeth seemed to be ascendant,
at any rate she was in the front row at the christening of Amalia's child
whereas the actual mother was relegated to the second row. Their

striving was more than personal because it helped to propel the sombre milieu of the Dutch Republic into the constellations of frivolous rivalry associated with the royal courts of Europe.

When his luck turned in 1660, Charles left for England from Scheveningen. On landing he immediately found himself surrounded by servants and hangers-on, including such vital members of staff as the keepers of the royal cormorants. And as soon as he was back on the English throne his louche behaviour and that of the libertines he favoured as courtiers took by storm the already compromised sobriety of Protector Cromwell's entourage. Charles's reign ended with grandiose plans for a Versailles at Winchester, a monster remaining largely unbuilt at his death. What little of it was left finally burned down in the nineteenth century.

The Winter Queen sailed for England too, taking up residence in the Earl of Craven's London house. Her lifestyle helped to ratify the stylishness that monarchy loved. Craven established a country residence for her at Hampstead Marshall, Berkshire, and built her a hunting lodge way out on the downs at Ashdown House, next to the Wiltshire border. This house, with its rooftop platform from which deer hunting and hare coursing could be watched, is tall and upright. It is beautifully symmetrical and is usually described as like an Amsterdam townhouse, which seems about right despite the setting of a downland park. 'A very singularly situated mansion, a sort of "Oasis in the desert"', a nineteenth-century observer called it. In support of the contention that Elizabeth and the Earl of Craven were lovers, the suggestion has been made that the house sports numerous phallic symbols. Obviously semiotics lies in the eye of the beholder and I cannot read the signs myself. If Ashdown were truly a coded message from a besotted Craven to the Winter Queen it went unread, because she died in 1662 before ever visiting the house. Others, though, could fill her role at court and her competition with Amalia Solms at the Hague was replaced in England by the rivalry between two of Charles's mistresses, Barbara Palmer, Countess of Castlemaine, and Louise de Kerouaille, Duchess of Portsmouth. They perpetuated extravagance at the peak of the social pyramid.

Luxury had somehow to be paid for. As far as the workings of the state and public finances went, the unreliable machinery of government was likely to respond by imposing the equivalent of hypothecated taxation, which is to say raising money for specific ends. A comprehensive tax system was administratively too difficult for any mid-seventeenth century regime. We saw this illustrated at Beaminster, Dorset, where the catastrophic loss from a fire set by Royalist troops in 1644 was made good when Parliament obliged a Royalist landowner to foot the bill. After the Restoration, money was raised more systematically by means of a hearth tax but because this could not be introduced until Michaelmas, 1662, the device first employed was a levy called 'The Free and Voluntary Present to King Charles II'. Records of this survive and have been transcribed for Oxfordshire. Voluntary is as voluntary does and in effect the gift was a loyalty test; most of the better-off ensured they passed by paying up. The hearth tax itself was 'farmed out', guaranteeing the king revenue. The 'farmers' had an incentive to make sure the tax was collected in order to recoup more than the payment they had advanced.

The Restoration court was an expensive one but the government of which it was the apex offered security to those with wealth, whatever their allegiances may have been before 1660. Many former Parliamentarians adapted to it, alarmed as were all but the most hardened ideologues by the near-chaos in the final stages of the Interregnum. Under both Parliamentary and Royalist regimes there were numerous instances of the malleability of behaviour and expressed attitudes, that is to say there was preference falsification. Senior officers of the Commonwealth might secretly espouse the old ways, as when Nicholas Taylor of Presteigne, Radnorshire, had four of his children privately baptised by an ordained clergyman between 1654 and 1660. Much of this shifty behaviour was for the sake of clinging onto or recovering family estates. The case of the Roman Catholic Duke of Beaufort makes the point. He converted to Protestantism to save his estates and he and his wife tried to keep their heads down during the last years of the Interregnum, though without wholly succeeding. They fell under grave suspicion of involvement in the so-called Gloucestershire Plot of 1659 which was meant to coincide with two other revolts, one in Surrey involving Sir Edward Hopton of Stretton Grandison, Herefordshire, and Booth's more developed uprising in Cheshire. When the Beaufort house at Badminton was searched for weapons all that were found however were the pistols carried by the Duke's servants when collecting his rents in Wales. That in itself was a comment on the times. In 1660 the Duke quickly reconsidered his cautious approach to politics, believing that an overt show of loyalty to the king would now be the best way to protect his extensive property.

As another example of changes in allegiance by those with great property to lose, note the behaviour of William Cooke of Highnam

Court, Gloucestershire, a war-damaged house that he restored in 1658. He made the house a notable example of Puritan Classicism. Unlike his father and brothers, for theirs was a prominent Puritan family, he had not taken up arms against Charles I but did accept local office under the Commonwealth. This he continued after 1660, having prudently signed the Gloucestershire Address of Welcome to Charles II. At the Restoration he made sure to hide away in the stable court the unctuous statue of Cromwell, described as half-nude, half-Roman, and posing as Hercules, which he had displayed over his south door. It was not given an airing again until 1920, two hundred and sixty years later.

Charles II was understandably wary of counter-plots and wished to keep track of former members of the Parliamentary forces. Regicides were often hunted down or they fled to eke out long, fearful lives in Calvinist Switzerland or Puritan New England. For a time, additions were made to the list of those excluded from amnesty but by and large retribution under the monarchy was limited, pragmatic or inconsistent. John Thurloe, although arrested for High Treason, was never tried and was released on the understanding that he would make his expertise available to Charles II's regime. Unton Croke was put on a £4000 bond for peaceable behaviour yet his elder son became Recorder and M.P. for Oxford, having reinvented himself to keep his place. Government agents ordinarily concentrated on the most martial suspects. Yet after some harsh treatment immediately after the Restoration, many Cromwellians, even a handful of regicides, did get their land back. It was one thing to refrain from punishing one's enemies – a tactical rather than genuinely personal decision - but another to sweeten one's friends. Rewards to Royalists came indirectly from the 'cavalier parliament' of the 1660s which was active in conferring pensions beyond the monarch's own rather selective generosity: it was alternatively known as the 'Pensioners' Parliament'.

The Parliamentarians could not know how gentle Charles would be towards those who had not specifically signed his father's death warrant and now made shift to be seen in a good light, sometimes even anticipating the Restoration. In the Restoration year itself, a trice before the actual event, a marriage was arranged between Edmund Prideaux's daughter and William Morice, who soon became secretary of state to the new king. This secured the Prideaux family a royal pardon. No doubt it helped that Edmund Prideaux had resigned as Solicitor-General rather than be involved in prosecuting Charles I, but he had compromised himself afterwards by agreeing to become Cromwell's Attorney-General.

Friend and foe often lived close together in tiny and relatively remote parishes which, the intricacies of English geography being what they are, can be separated even today by the lie of the land and the dominance of certain roads. This indicates the salience of local studies. Neighbours with different views might be ignored but relationships could be more fraught than giving them the cold shoulder. During the years of war the treatment of losers had sometimes been harsh. Puritans flung the aged vicar of Steeple Langford, Wiltshire, out into the snow and two of his sons who were captured in the Penruddock Rising were sold to Barbados as slaves only four or five years before Charles II regained the throne. If we look specifically at the Bourne valley, which runs down to Salisbury and from whose parishes Penruddock drew many supporters, we can see that civil conflict made rural society claustrophobic.

Thomas Rutter, Penruddock's so-called Quartermaster-General, came from West Cholderton near Newton Tony; he was searched for after the Rising but could not be found. It is even said that General Monck, who engineered the return of the Monarchy, was living only three or four miles away in Idmiston manor when negotiations about the Restoration began, although the chronology seems not to fit. We have already seen that Robert Wallop, the regicide, who had served on the commission to try the Joneses after the Rising, held Allington manor, a mere mile from their estate at Newton Tony. To cap the concentration of activity along this one little Wiltshire valley, John Rede, a Parliamentary colonel and prominent Baptist, lived at Porton, a hamlet of Idmiston where the family of the incumbent, the Bowles, were strong Royalists.

During the eighteenth-century, a Bowles analysed the Idmiston parish registers and remarked on the great number of non-parishioners who were married there. This he attributed to Rede's influence; he thought individuals from remote places may have met first at Baptist gatherings in Rede's Birdlyme Farm. The reader may tire of the ironies but Bowles was undertaking a piece of social science research to communicate to Daines Barrington. Barrington was the correspondent to whom Gilbert White addressed part of *The Natural History of Selborne* and his ancestors were Puritans who obtained their estate at Shrivenham through their connection with John Wildman. Plainly, asperities had softened over the years between politically different families like the Barringtons and the Bowles.

The viciousness of the Civil War and the subsequent persecution of Quakers and Nonconformists gave way to de facto tolerance. Some

Puritans even sat in Charles's first Parliament and the families of many former Roundheads settled back with ease into the ranks of the consolidated gentry. The landowner class was happy to restrict future disputes to contesting for seats in Parliament via noisy, boozy elections that soon involved bribery - but not via armed conflict. Details of the post-Restoration picture are mixed and by telescoping time and forgetting we have the benefit of hindsight it is easy to make the transition seem milder than it was. In reality the generations after the Restoration witnessed alarms like the 'Fifteen and the 'Forty-five in the eighteenth century. Nevertheless the best generalisation remains the one indicated by the title of J. H. Plumb's book, *The Growth of Political Stability in England, 1675-1725*. This captures the trend, although the basis of stability was surely laid even earlier, in those Siamese-twin decades, the 1650s and 1660s.

A useful way of looking at the transition from civil violence to relative tranquillity is to consider it partly as a process whereby politics was sublimated in religion. This was no absolute happening or iron-clad equation but the approach is informative. Obviously religious discord had been conspicuous, to say the least, in the conflicts of the mid-seventeenth century and had been brewing for a long time before that. It had been instrumental in sundering society, especially in the early stages of open conflict. Religious differences were part and parcel of political affiliations and the rhetoric and culture of the age meant that all sides were convinced, or strove to appear convinced, that they were performing the Lord's work. There was much talk of Christ, though behind His throne just as much worship of mammon. The conjunction of religion and politics had turned out to be fatal because, when the two were conflated, the stabilisers of cross-cutting diversity were pulled away and attitudes became positively tribal.

Insurgents and defenders of the status quo both displayed unbridled self-confidence; to each, their morality and self-interest seemed to reinforce one another. An equation of religion and politics certainly persisted after the Restoration and some self-proclaimed Christians continued to be unforgiving. This is not surprising when cruelty and persecution, death and destruction, were so recent. Seth Ward, the arrogant Bishop of Salisbury from 1667, compiled a list of people whose attitudes in the 1650s had not been to his taste; he made sure that Nonconformists were given an uncomfortable time. Again, this is not surprising, if only because the spoils of victory included the patronage that stemmed from ejecting Nonconformist preachers who had acquired Anglican livings under the Puritans and thereafter reassigning their places to right-thinking men. Despite all this, the divisions did not crack right open again. Those who were averse to the Church of England retreated into what may be termed sectarianism, without further plotting or at any rate without another Rising. Like the political stability of which Plumb wrote, the dampening of religious conflict was a mark of the age and is a puzzle to interpret.

The first sect to suffer from Cavalier vengeance had been the Society of Friends. Militias were ordered to ride out and break up its gatherings. In 1663 one troop dug up the graves in the Quaker burial ground at Manton, just west of Marlborough, a gruesome event that provoked noisy remonstrations from local people, not just from the Quakers themselves. It has to be borne in mind that many Quakers had served in the Parliamentary army and were not inevitably the quietists the sect later became. Quakers rejected hierarchy but could not deny having their own officer class: there were gentlemen among them. Giles Fettiplace used to travel by coach and horses from his estate at Coln St Aldwyn, Gloucestershire, to the Cirencester meeting. In the immediate post-Restoration years, Quakers could understandably be feared as potential threats. Fears reached the fanciful when the government came to believe that the Quakers were buying up the best horses, taken to be a sure sign of a coming Rising. Apprehensions on those lines were not completely silly at times of disturbance and uncertainty but the breaking up of Quaker meetings and the punishments laid on them were as plainly the hysteria of bullies as they were instruments of public order. In January 1661, Marmaduke Langdale was writing anxiously from Yorkshire, asking whether he should bear down on the Quakers as hard as his neighbours wished. That year a supposed 5,000 Quakers were imprisoned by Anglican magistrates.

To jump ahead to the eighteenth century, political stability and the economy's attractions had within a generation undermined any sense that the Quakers were threats. Those of the gentry who had belonged to the Society of Friends began sliding back to the Church of England. Few Giles Fettiplaces were to be found any longer. Fettiplace's son-in-law, John Bellers, who followed him as lord of the manor of Coln St. Aldwyn, and whose writings were admired by Marx, began lamenting the loss of fervour among his fellow Quakers well before his own death in 1725. Ordinary Quakers busied themselves making money, using the unfamiliar business device of honest dealing. In the market towns the Quakers became prosperous, mundane tradesmen, including brewers. They became members of the borough establishment and took their turn as mayor. Like many of the Nonconformists, the Quakers permitted religious practices to subdue their political activism and expressed their religious energies in commercial bustle.

About the date of the Penruddock Rising there had been a big gathering of Baptists at Porton, close to Newton Tony. They too were often former Cromwellian soldiers. They met in the large hall of John Rede's Birdlyme farmhouse, where iii people from Hampshire and Wiltshire gathered on 3rd April, 1655, only three weeks after Penruddock had captured nearby Salisbury. The meetings ceased sometime between 1660 and 1672, when the persecution of nonconformists was at its height. The post-Restoration Clarendon Code required nonconformist ministers to swear not only religious fealty but a political oath certifying they would not endeavour to overturn the government. The Five Mile Act excluded nonconformists from worshipping in the towns. Their adaptation to this stricture meant that certain places which fell outside the radius of five miles became great centres of nonconformity, though Porton was not one of them. One village that did satisfy the requirement was Avebury, which became a great nonconformist centre in Wiltshire because it was situated just far enough from a whole ring of towns. During and after the 1660s, ministers ejected from their churches because they would not subscribe to the articles of the established church took to walking astonishing distances to preach to the faithful in places like Avebury. In order to hear them, large congregations assembled from almost as far.

At the Restoration, Charles II had been obliged to find a way of coping with the Parliamentary leaders. The costs of imprisoning them all would have been too high and risked sparking renewed conflict or at a minimum slowing economic recovery. Charles was too astute to risk that. Not all of the most prominent were easily reconciled and minor Roundheads were less so, but their proscribed political views found expression in non-conforming religion and even that was controlled by law. Nonconformist gatherings understandably continued to be looked on with suspicion, particularly if they were as large as the ones at Avebury or drew people from great distances. Those who attended might be getting together for worship but equally it might be feared they were plotting. Some may indeed have wished to plot but their grumbling came to naught, their numbers eroded by those among them who preferred to settle for a peaceful existence.

Two of the leading occupants of the borderland of religion and politics may be considered here. First, Nathaniel Fiennes, who owned the Newton Tony estate which previously belonged to Francis Jones. Fiennes's reputation was dubious and one of his descendants has remarked in print that his contemporaries found him tiresome. Clarendon laughed at him for turning tail at the gates of Worcester and he had almost been shot by Cromwell for surrendering Bristol to the Royalists in 1643. The Earl of Essex secured his release and Fiennes went overseas but was back in 1646 and eventually made peace with the Protector, to the point of becoming his close confidant. Fiennes's second wife was the daughter of the Roundhead Colonel, Richard Whitehead of Tytherley. She hosted a conventicle in the house at Newton Tony. James White, who had been given the rectory there at the Restoration, committed suicide in 1661 and it has been speculated that this was because he had come into conflict with Fiennes. Whether or not this is fair is unclear; of the Fiennes couple the wife was the more ardently religious and White was anyhow battling wider nonconformist activity in the parish. He faced articulate opposition because John Crofts, chaplain to Fiennes's wife, had been chaplain to Alice Lisle at Ellingham, Hampshire, where two hundred people 'of the meaner sort' attended the Presbyterian conventicle.

Four houses in Allington, the next village to Newton Tony, were used for Presbyterian meetings in 1669, a year in which large numbers of Baptists were attending meetings in towns and villages in the region and when a fine was levied for the holding of a conventicle at Newton Tony. The following year, during the brief Indulgence issued by the King, two houses in the village (neither of them the Fiennes' mansion) were certified as dissenters' meeting houses, one Congregational, the other Presbyterian. This illustrates the fragmentation of alternatives to the established church and hence the declining chances of unified resistance to the Crown. Nathaniel Fiennes died in 1669, but in May 1672 John Crofts was licenced as a Congregational teacher in one of the two village houses and a few days later he was licenced as a Presbyterian teacher in the house of Frances Fiennes, which was presumably the mansion. There was also a Baptist church at nearby Idmiston, which village was the home of a yeoman who had been executed for his part in the Penruddock Rising. All these places lay within very few miles of one another, derisorily short distances given how far people were then willing to walk to meetings.

The religious activities of another prominent Parliamentarian, Bulstrode Whitelocke, offer a parallel. He retreated after the Restoration to his mansion at Chilton Foliat, Wiltshire, just over the county boundary from Hungerford, Berkshire. One hundred people met in the conventicle in his mansion. In 1670, following the severe Conventicle Act, people from Ramsbury and Pusey sought Whitelocke's legal advice about what to do. He went out of his way to remain friends with the local Anglican vicar in the hope of ensuring that the man's successor would be another moderate, even though at the same time he was trying to build a broad front of dissent based on Chilton Park. He had a personal word with the Bishop of Winchester to influence the appointment. The Bishop was the arch-Royalist, George Morley, who had held the living at Minal into the war years, illustrating the strange cross-currents of the age. The conventicle in Whitelocke's house ceased on his death in 1675 but by then this did not matter much, since following the Indulgence of 1672 people from nearby Hungerford had sought to register their own meeting.

Whitelocke had been heavily fined at the Restoration. Although part of the fine may have been revoked, he certainly disbursed great sums to keep his name off the list of those responsible for executing Charles I. Despite the cost of the bribes, he was still rich and his continued sectarian activity, which might be seen as the residue of the Cromwellian politico-religious programme, did not preclude him from making commercial investments. He stood surety for the agricultural pioneer, Jethro Tull of Prosperous Farm, Shalbourne, which is not far from Chilton or Hungerford. Tull was broke at the time but unlike Tull money tended to stick to Whitelocke hands. There is an early eighteenth-century plaque in the parish church at Chilton Foliat, not in a nonconformist chapel, to Whitelocke's grandson, who died a bachelor and left his fortune to his nieces.

By the mid-eighteenth century, nonconformity was a feature of those settlements in the diocese of Salisbury that were not under the thumb of great landlords or powerful clergy. According to the *Wiltshire Archaeological Magazine* for 2013, half of Wiltshire smallholder communities possessed a meeting house, compared with only six per cent of parishes dominated by landed oligarchs. The situation was similar in Berkshire. Nonconformist sects tended to contain the more thoughtful and independent-minded members of the population, as opposed to people obliged by the local hierarchies to attend the Church of England, or who attended out of habit or self-interest. Later, the Wesleyans were the ones who refused sugar in order not to support slavery, whereas the lists of slave owners who were compensated for their losses at emancipation in the early nineteenth century contain numbers of Anglican clerics. And it was in the established church that pews could be had for rent, while squires tended not only to have their own pews but to have privileged access to them, witness the door behind the pulpit at Keevil, Wiltshire. Even in the twenty-first century the owner of Faringdon House, Berkshire (now Oxfordshire) inherited her own pew.

Religious strife can be made to sound a matter of contests between alternative, rational interpretations of Christianity. In reality, the seventeenth-century conflict between Anglicans and the nonconformists and Quakers was not merely sublimated politics but was also played out against a background of superstition that was only slowly fading. Two regional examples may be cited. One was the episode at Fairford, Gloucestershire, where in 1660 meetings of the Independents had been forcibly broken up, as such gatherings often were. Almost immediately, the house and barn of the unsympathetic landowner were invaded by frogs and flies. This sparked a pamphlet exchange and was depicted by some as divine retribution, whereas it was plainly a seasonal spread of caddis flies and frogs from the nearby river. Frogs still come up from the river every February. A second episode was the case the next year, 1661, of a ghostly drummer infesting the house at North Tidworth on the Hampshire-Wiltshire border belonging to a cousin of the Thomas Mompesson who had raised a mounted force for Penruddock. Visitors who should have known better attributed this hoax to a poltergeist. It was an age of 'anxious speculation' related to the tensions of the time, when even some of the educated gave credence to fraudulent and supposedly supernatural events.

All this shows that what was happening in respect of sectarian disputes was complicated and changed over time. The saga may be a reflection of England's long drawn-out, incomplete, Reformation. The continued presence in the country of Roman Catholics, despite all persecution, provoked fears of a re-catholicisation that were shared by Anglicans and non-conformists alike and conduced to long-term religious unease. Yet after 1660 Puritan discontent was retreating from provocative secular claims into more single-minded spiritual expression. Even that line of retreat was not easy at first. The victory of the Cavaliers meant that their enemies were initially excluded from political life and hampered in their religious observances. The thaw took some time to arrive.

The differences over religion may strike modern readers as Little Ender-Big Ender disputes and the existence of conflict among professing Christians as almost tantamount to blasphemy. The fact that disputes remained worrying is partly explained by the extent of the preceding turmoil and partly by the way that religious adherence could be code for politics – an equation high-lighted by the fact that in 1658 congregations openly labelled Royalist were meeting in the City of London. This is not to claim that every religious conflict of the era reflected material interests or personal ambitions; church historians would reject that over-simple interpretation. Consider William Dowsing, who with his assistants did so much in 1644 to destroy what Puritans considered to be the superstitious ornamentation of Suffolk churches. However destructively zealous he was, Dowsing was without doubt a learned and patently sincere autodidact. On the other hand, there was quite soon sufficient backsliding to disillusion him and permit the forces of Mammon to adulterate his crusade.

By the end of the seventeenth century public affairs settled into primarily rhetorical discord. Nonconformists tended by and large to concentrate on work and business, paving the way for economic growth. Anglicans on the other hand were loud exponents of the symbolism of conjoined church and state, as is plain in the prayer book put out in 1722 by the publisher to the king. It contained overtly political illustrations such as Guy Fawkes watched by the Almighty's eye, the martyrdom of Charles I, and the Restoration of Charles II. Prayers on facing pages call for preservation from the secret contriving and hellish malice of Popery, and more in a like unchristian vein. Yet by that date the various sects were following separate and parallel paths unsullied by the previous violence.

'The ecclesiastical history of the period is simply a record of confusion', says *The Cambridge Modern History*. Never was a truer word written. Confusion had resolved itself into future centuries of worship segregated by class. Typical nonconformists lived apart from Anglicans in chapel communities that barely interacted with the rich and ceased to challenge the authorities directly, though nationally they formed such

Royalist triumphalism in an Anglican prayer book of 1722, apparently still in use at Shobdon, Herefordshire, in 2016

a large community they did not think of themselves as isolated. The leaders of society having fused again in one social tier, some of their leading opponents joined them because they could not beat them. Many among the Puritan elite soon conformed to Anglican norms and others followed within a generation or two. In the eighteenth century their children or grand-children, doubtless horrified at ancestral tales of war and destruction, increasingly discovered the attractions of shifting to the established church, abandoning the chapels and meeting houses to the working class. The families of professionals also tended to move away from the chapel.

Nonconformist energies were released in the reign of William III (1694-1702), when many hundreds, perhaps over one thousand, meeting houses and chapels were built. Energies that did not go into commerce tended to be diverted inwards, towards competition for adherents among splintering sects and the founding of new ranks of chapels where rising tradesmen could come to the fore and achieve personal prominence in new tiers of worship. In the Anglican world, on the other hand, assertions of loyalty to the reigning monarch, or monarchy in general, became routine, with the royal arms displayed in churches and the insistence of many wall plaques that the dead came from old and above all loyal families. Church attendance by the tenants and servants of conservative landowners was monitored; chapel attendance by the employees of nonconformist manufacturers could be monitored too. Rich proprietors were in a position to do virtually what they pleased with church buildings; they could build new ones and demolish or threaten to demolish the old. Richard's Castle on the border of Herefordshire and Shropshire is an example. There the landowner opened a new church in the 1890s and was barely dissuaded from pulling down its marvellous fourteenth-century predecessor. Secular power and ecclesiastical symbolism commonly manifested themselves in private gateways to churchyards from the grounds of the manors next door; separate entrances to the churches themselves, as at Sherborne and Horton in Gloucestershire; and separate pews to keep rich and poor at arms' length. Occasional distinct churches too, as at Tetbury, where the Victorian inheritors of the Restoration settlement brazenly built a 'little church for the poor.' At Shrivenham not one but three private paths led to the church, a structure that houses the expensive floor slab of the arch-Leveller, John Wildman.

7

ANIMAL FARM AND ELITE SETTLEMENT

I N THE MOST striking thesis I read while doing research for this book, Gilbert Farthing quotes a contemporary pamphlet asserting that King and Parliament had only one quarrel, 'namely, whose slaves the people shall be.' This was by no means too cynical. The following centuries of income and wealth inequality, domination of the countryside by the squires and subjugation of ordinary people show it. Their suppressed talent burst forth among a proportion of those who escaped to the cities or the more democratic of the colonies. In the nature of things, we cannot measure the extent of rural humiliation but one feature was the continued exercise of *droit de seigneur* which might be thought to have ended in the Middle Ages. We can never know how widespread the practice was but with vast discrepancies of power and the everyday subjugation of women, resistance must often have been fruitless. Of the wide-scale abuse of maid servants over the centuries there is not the slightest doubt.

When his landowning godfather died at eighty-nine, Ashley Cooper wrote that 'he borrowed to carress his neighbours' wives and daughters' and in all his 'walks' (sections of Cranbourne Chase) 'there was not a woman of the degree of a yeoman's wife or under, and under the age of forty, but it was her own fault if he was not intimately acquainted with her.' That was in Dorset. In Victorian Wales a visiting judge was startled to be told by a Lord Lieutenant that the servants were the fruit of his own loins. A highly circumstantial and remarkably recent account relating to twentieth-century Northamptonshire is to be found in Byron Rogers's *The Green Lane to Nowhere*. The illegitimate offspring went away when they grew up and never came back.

Whichever side won in the great civil conflict, few in the elite wanted their own power and privileges removed. They had wished to abolish arbitrary rule by Charles I as well as his popish flavouring of religion. They aimed for a constitutional monarchy, which they came to agree was the most desirable and durable form of government. In other respects the Civil War struggle was almost pointless. The Royalist Earl of Berkshire plaintively declared, 'Nobody can tell what we have fought about all this while.' If the Earl of Berkshire from his close viewpoint could not decide what the Civil War was about, maybe with the advantage of hindsight we can spot some pattern or purpose. The enormous dispersion of unrecorded personal decisions nevertheless makes it unlikely that any discernible pattern remains to be found at a general level. What we do see is an autoimmune disease of the power structure. The sickness began as perfectly understandable resistance to Charles I's would-be authoritarianism but got out of hand and ended with the system fighting itself.

There were three nexuses at the relevant social level, which was that of the officer class. One was the old landed aristocrats with great estates; the second was the big London merchants, often with landed estates too; and the third was the country landowners, whose capital had also frequently derived from London, even from trade, though at early enough dates for them to pass as to the manor born. London connections and inter-marriages ensured a considerable overlap of families. Everybody rubbed along together until their differences in religion and politics polarised and they divided into Cavalier and Roundhead categories, on which basis they fell out disastrously. Even so, both factions retained *ex officio* membership of the ruling class. During the war Levellers had come to suspect that some of the Parliamentary leaders were willing to temporise and treat with their peers on the other side.

A telling observation about class relations is that, despite the wars and despite their greed, some Roundhead landowners in the 1650s hesitated to snap up the estates of neighbours who were bowing under the weight of fines. Neighbouring owners were too often their relatives by marriage or had at least been their friends. Neutral or formerly Royalist gentry avoided prosecuting the laws of Commonwealth or Protectorate sedulously. The surveying of landed estates to set the level of fines was not carried out with rigour. Rural history during the 1650s accordingly fell into three phases. At first under the Protectorate the moderate gentry soon stopped grousing; their loyalty was to peace in their home districts. Secondly came the Penruddock Rising and in its wake rule by the Major-Generals. This intensified the bad blood; stern taxation and suppression of sports meetings and other gatherings were deeply resented. Yet the sway of the Major-Generals lasted only from August, 1655, to January, 1657, which meant, thirdly, that in little more than eighteen months the old gentry were again accepting local office and under Richard Cromwell were actively restoring or developing their own estates.

Only operators like John Wildman had speculated extensively in forfeited estates, although it is true he was often fronting for others. The purchase of Francis Jones's estate in 1656 by Nathaniel Fiennes might seem another exception to any rule of forbearance. But although Fiennes' father had held a position in Wiltshire and he had himself married a Roundhead colonel's daughter from only just over the Hampshire border, ten miles or so away, Nathaniel had never been a neighbour of the Joneses. A twentieth-century Fiennes described him as typical of the country gentry who supported parliament but 'with one foot in a conservative past whose constitutional rights and liberties they fought to restore from the innovative autocracy of the King, without any wish to endanger their own position in society.'

This was well put. 'Without wishing to endanger their own position' is the default phrase. Roundhead grandees like the great lawyer officials, Nathaniel Fiennes and Bulstrode Whitelocke, were concerned to maintain the rule of law in their own interest or the rights of property. They were 'traditionalist Cromwellians' who saw the person of Oliver Cromwell as a bulwark against social revolution. They upheld the law, despite hesitations about where the source of legal authority might lie in the absence of a monarch and despite the gamble involved in those times for anyone who submitted his affairs to the decisions of the judiciary, the impartiality of which they knew was compromised. Cromwell appeared an incomplete substitute for royalty to any but the naïve, the ideologues, or the sycophantic, but law itself was too useful a social glue to be jettisoned by those with much to lose and whose deep pockets meant they could afford access to the courts. Laws and the forms of state went some way to disguise the political bargaining that was the true and ultimate decider.

Roundheads were far from uniformly ascetic or gentle people. Consider the family of Edmund Ludlow, a prominent regicide from Maiden Bradley, Wiltshire, which had already acquired an 'evil reputation' as encroaching landlords. One of them bore this out by pulling down tenants' houses. Another strong Parliamentarian in the same county, Sir John Danvers, deposed that his own brother was a Royalist 'malignant' in order to have his will set aside. By the candidly named 'Division of Plunder' of 1644, Danvers also managed to exclude his sister from the family estate. He was deep in debt himself through extravagance on a scale that might have shamed the most flamboyant Cavalier, having spent exorbitant sums on ornamental gardens at West Lavington, Wiltshire. The national pork barrel was dipped into continually, Cromwell granting favours like an eastern potentate. For instance he gave Robert Jenner, a member of the Long Parliament, the right to carve a new ecclesiastical parish called Marston Meysey, Wiltshire, out of neighbouring Meysey Hampton, Gloucestershire. Cromwell also gave permission to John Dutton, who although a Royalist was a personal friend, to stock his new park at Sherborne, Gloucestershire, with deer from Wychwood Forest. Bestowing rights like these was the means of cementing alliances practised by monarchs and dictators throughout history, regardless of the fact that typical appreciations of Cromwell portray him as less venal than most.

Cromwell had the miniaturist, Samuel Cooper, paint him 'warts and all', together with the patches of scalp exposed beneath what Simon Schama calls his lank comb-over. The idea was that candid nationalism would bind the loyalty of citizens better than the cosmetic flattery mandated by the vanity of kings. Recall that Elizabeth had commanded that she be painted only as an agelessly young Queen. Cromwell's self-denying ordinance did not last. He was personally ambivalent about the symbols of majesty but his adherents pressed the usefulness of such baubles on him. Antonia Fraser discovered an unambiguous expression of this in advice given by the Duke of Newcastle to the young Prince Charles before the Civil War; drums, trumpets, rich furniture, lots of flunkeys... 'even the wisest... shall shake off his wisdom, and shake for fear of it, for this is the mist cast before us, and masters the commonwealth.' Nor did Cromwell fail to perceive the advantages of marrying members of his own family to his leading lieutenants. He went further and contemplated permitting family marriages with the nation's high and mighty, including royalty.

Cromwell's household, especially his daughters, were not immune from consuming the trinkets with which the rich like to surround themselves. The sober dress and manners associated with Puritanism were undermined. Earthly pleasures began to seep back and by 1654 women were reverting to painting their faces. The females luxuriating a few years later in the complex anthropology of Charles II's harlot court were not the ones breaking the norms of fashion history. The real break had come early in Puritan rule, ornamentation and display having been set aside only briefly when the frivolity of the rich and powerful was interrupted in the late 1640s and early 1650s. At that time society's leaders adopted Puritan styles but only for a short space and even then the Puritan Minimalism or Classicism of their mansions was a cryptic form of ostentation. The licentious Restoration court was thus scarcely more than an exaggerated rebound to the long-term trend. Personal display is always hard to suppress. Never mind what men are wearing, it is female adornment that should be watched, for it is there that conventions are first flouted: they were in Nazi Germany, they are in modern Iran, and Jung Chang's *Wild Swans* reveals that tiny signs of individualism crept into Chinese dress at the very height of Maoism.

Music, dancing, theatre and portraiture also returned in the 1650s. Cromwell, who liked that sort of music, had the Magdalen College organ taken to Hampton Court for his personal delight. The unsold residue of the King's furniture, paintings and tapestries was installed in Cromwell's own residences. He granted his mother a Westminster Abbey funeral, lighted by hundreds of torches. Whatever their protestations, the prizes aspired to by those members of Roundhead society who set the tone matched the sweets that had been revelled in by the Stuart courts. Many saw the personal advantage of being heard greeting Cromwell as 'Your Highness', or at least recognised the value of not seeming to stand aside. Parliamentarians may have differed politically and religiously from Royalists, but socially they were often much the same people, sometimes exactly the same people, though joined by a number of time-servers and social climbers for whom the regime made an opening in the way that new regimes do. The Major-Generals, Cromwell's creatures, were prominent among the parvenu group and predictably enough tended to be the most insecure, vindictive and unbending. As far as their venal colleagues were concerned, extremists like the Major-Generals performed the role of useful idiots. This stiffening by high-minded ideologues had its day but became irritating to the people at large and the gentry in particular, given the suppressing of Maypoles and Christmas and, when it suited, horse-racing too. That Christmas Day was not a public holiday in Scotland until 1958 and Boxing Day not until 1974 are said to have been Cromwellian legacies. Other affronts soon faded.

Corruption was endemic and the regimes of the Interregnum were not the ones to curb it. Bulstrode Whitelocke admitted that under the Protectorate side-payments had exceeded his official earnings. Like all office holders, he exacted levies from those supplicating favours. Royalist government after the Restoration was personalised and corrupt too – Whitelocke, who had sixteen children to support, had to lay out a fortune in bribes to escape being 'excepted' from Charles II's general amnesty. The bribes were worth it since not being amnestied would probably have meant being executed. Meanwhile he was casually referring to the 'common people', which like 'mean persons' was a standard disparagement at the time. Despite his politics (he had been Cromwell's ambassador to Sweden) and religion (conventicles were held in his mansion at Chilton Foliat, Wiltshire), his family continued to do well financially into the next century.

The 1640s and 1650s saw endless tussles about the desirability of different forms of government and the means of putting them into effect. All this betokened a society functionally and socially not enormously different from the monarchical one it replaced or the one that was to follow. With only a fringe of discontented exceptions, continuity rather than change was the theme at the landowner level. Leading Puritans were thoroughly status-conscious – no Levellers they. They shared the 'fleering contempt' for inferiors displayed by the Cavaliers. Unton Croke described some Penruddock supporters in class terms as 'contemptible persons', just as Cromwell said they were 'mean persons.' When Whitelocke was belatedly informed that he had been chosen as a candidate for an election he complained that he had learned this only when 'a plain country fellow in mean habit' arrived at his chambers in the Inner Temple to tell him. Henry Marten, in what at first sight seemed a democratic gesture, forbade the people to stand bare, meaning hatless, to do fealty to their lords at the law sessions, but this insistence on his own desires made him as much a bully as any Tory squire.

The Cromwellian regime had attempted to compile a list of its potential enemies, constables being required to forward returns of all those who in their parishes had borne arms against the Parliament. Alleged Royalists were divided into three categories, at least on paper. Anyone who had participated in a plot was to have two-thirds of his estate appropriated, anyone who had spoken in favour of the Stuarts was to be jailed or banished (though their estates were not forfeit), and those who had fought on the king's side were to be heavily fined. Severe penalties attached to offences such as keeping an ejected minister of the church in one's house. Bounty hunters and former Parliamentary soldiers questing for 'concealed land' that might evade taxation were soon a 'plague'. Royalists who had no property or could not give an account of themselves were to be transported, meaning they were to be sent to the West Indies to labour in the sugar plantations. These fines, penalties and restrictions read as if the regime operated an efficient bureaucracy, although in practice this proved not to be true at all.

Despite the fine talk under the Protectorate, an acquisitiveness that might be destabilising was tempting to many. Society needed to be steered by formal rules that were not wholly constraining but would act as long stops. Cromwell personally may not have seemed excessively concerned with riches, although the fact that he accepted Parliamentary grants of land generating considerable rents in a long list of counties perhaps says otherwise. Leading Roundheads who were in a position to do so, far from being unwilling to spend out on inessentials like country mansions, consolidated their possessions with almost indecent haste. Once the king was dead, they built themselves splendid houses in the restrained style called Puritan Minimalism or Puritan Classicism. In *Architecture without Kings: The Rise of Puritan Classicism under Cromwell*, Tim Mowl and Brian Earnshaw describe the style as having an 'ostentatious humility of design.' Ostentatious is the operative word. The speed with which those opposed to the king celebrated their new dominance was remarkable, as was the way in which they seized economic opportunity. New or restored market houses went up very soon after the king's execution, for example at Faringdon, then in Berkshire, and Ross-on-Wye, Herefordshire.

Too many Roundheads to be dismissed as an errant fringe grasped at material reward, confirming that they and the Cavaliers were what Gore Vidal labelled the Republicans and Democrats in modern America - members of the same Property Party. They acted under a cloak of legalism which they felt had the merit of sanctifying property rights. Viewed from a material perspective, the struggle between them sometimes devolved into a matter of who was to acquire the property of the losers. The long published inventory of Nathaniel Fiennes's possessions at Newton Tony shows that rich Parliamentarians profited from the Interregnum and many kept their great possessions afterwards.

During the 1650s, Spymaster Thurloe, who is described as not abnormally corrupt, had become a rich landowner. He built Wisbech

Castle, Cambridgeshire, and considered buying Anvills near Hungerford
from his close colleague, Bulstrode Whitelocke. Anvills had belonged
to the Penruddock rebel, Thomas Curr, a Roman Catholic who had
lost much of his land through adhering to the monarchy. To note that
Thurloe was brother-in-law to the shady and exceedingly rich scrivener
(notary and money-lender), Martin Noel, may be the smear of guilt by
association but it may equally be a sign of the lack of scruples at the
heart of the regime. John Lisle, President of the High Court, rebuilt his
wife's seat at Moyles Court, Hampshire. Edmund Prideaux, Cromwell's
attorney-general, remodelled Forde Abbey, Dorset. Oliver St John built
Thorpe Hall, Huntingdonshire. And the poet, Edmund Waller, a Royalist
who had switched sides, returned from exile to praise Cromwell (they
were related) as nothing short of a new Augustus. Waller put up Hall
Barn, Beaconsfield, as 'a wonderful Dutch-inspired dolls' house', like
the Earl of Craven's slightly later Ashdown House. Both houses pre-
dated the vogue for things Dutch introduced under William III.

Until the Restoration settlement most Royalists waited in the
wings. The constitutional outcome was promoted by that influential part
of the Parliamentary elite who brought back a faintly humbled Charles
II. He gave them assurances against arbitrariness in the Declaration
of Breda and they were more or less content with his guarantees
against future abuses of Royal power. 'The satraps of Cromwell after a
brief struggle', said Hugh Trevor-Roper, 'sold out to a more traditional
authority.' Charles's indolent diversions, stroking a cat during meetings
about government business and stroking his mistresses on as many
occasions as possible, offered a less formal assurance that politically he
was unlikely to assert himself overmuch. That was not a completely fair
appraisal of his energy but Parliamentarians wished to believe it all the
same.

Once the Crown had been restored, society settled, or settled
back, into a pattern. It might be urged that the terms of the old radical
Agreement of the People were substantially met by the provisions of
1660 and 1688, provided one overlooks the fact that they were not
actually carried out and anyhow scarcely applied to the 'common
people'. As Farthing forcefully argues, it was not meant to do so. In
1649 the heads of the army had paid little serious attention to the
constitutional arrangements proposed, being more concerned with the
exercise of power. The version of the Agreement of the People which
appeared that year called for biennial parliaments elected through

proportional representation on a basis of manhood suffrage. It proposed to enfranchise the tradesmen class, though not including servants, wage earners or recipients of welfare. Government was to be by the House of Commons, without reference to monarch or House of Lords. Freedom of conscience and the press, the abolition of press gangs, equality before the law, trial by jury, free trade, no usury, no monopolies, no tithes, free primary education for all... in theory none of these stipulations could be altered by Parliament. But insofar as they have since been achieved (the agenda plainly remains unfinished), they took centuries to bring to fruition.

The most fly among the Puritans hastened to profit mightily from the sale of the century, which was the disposal of Charles's assets immediately after his execution. Colonel Hutchinson, governor of Nottingham Castle, was quick and clever with buying and reselling royal paintings. What is more he bought and resold erotic nudes of classical goddesses by Titian. His wife, more austere than he, implied that this was to keep the treasures in the country and block the capital flight that threatened to follow the King's death. It sounds self-justifying, for the paintings were resold to foreign envoys.

Despite their substantially shared origins and personal connections, the Puritan and Royalist elites were admittedly not quite Tweedledum and Tweedledee. Attitudes were matters of shading and overlap, evolving as time went on. Not all Puritans were humourless bigots and many opinions were represented among them. Cromwell's court may have been verging on the royal and its behaviour did become less restrictive with some speed, which is the fundamental point, but the overt sexualisation characteristic of Charles II's court did not surface in Oliver's day. The story is told that Charles used to despatch high-born ladies to Stonelands, near Burford, where rich girls were sent to have abortions, so that their offspring could not complicate succession to the throne. Enough complications arose with the bastards sired on Charles's acknowledged mistresses. But this statement may be sourness akin to earlier Royalist propaganda sneering at, say, the prudent housekeeping of Elizabeth Cromwell.

Despite the intensity with which those so inclined pursued politics, the possession of desirable skills and an accommodating mind could contrive to get itself rewarded by successive rulers of quite different views. In the religiously fraught sixteenth century two men who must have had very honeyed tongues were first Thomas Wendy of Haslingfield, Cambridge, who managed to act as physician to Henry VIII and attend on their deathbeds both Edward VI and Queen Mary, and secondly Thomas Gresham, who was financier and royal agent to Edward and (although initially removed as politically unreliable) served both Mary and Elizabeth in the same roles. The seventeenth century produced adroit individuals who almost matched their records. The portraitist, Peter Lely, painted, one after the other, Charles I, Oliver Cromwell, Richard Cromwell and Charles II, while Edmund Waller lived to do better, writing poems eulogising successively not only Charles I, Cromwell, and Charles II but James II too. John Glynne, though head of the commission in the Penruddock trials, ended in the service of Charles II. James Howell had moved from royalism to uncritical admiration of Cromwell but was still appointed historiographer-royal under Charles II, while the cryptographer, John Wallis, kept his Oxford chair. The tomb of Henry White at West Knoyle, Wiltshire, records that he was Messenger to the most eminent kings of England, James I, Charles I and 'our present soverayne Charles II'. Others in royal service similarly retained or regained their footing in more than one reign, for instance the grave of William Sakings at Great Livermere, Suffolk, records that he was 'forkner' (falconer) to Charles I, Charles II and James II. But White and Sakings were genuine Royalists and not temporisers.

Robert Whitehall, the Earl of Rochester's tutor, was in the slippery category. An avowed Royalist who had originally refused to submit to Oliver Cromwell, Whitehall was nevertheless a familiar of one of the Protector's many cousins, the M.P. and regicide, Richard Ingoldsby, and soon succeeded in securing a fellowship at Merton College. Whitehall thereafter wrote sycophantic verse addressed to Oliver and Richard Cromwell. Ingoldsby himself supported both Cromwells but claimed Oliver had literally forced him to put his hand to Charles I's death warrant. He subsequently switched his support to Monck, thereby becoming one of the rare regicides to be pardoned; he was actually knighted at Charles II's coronation in 1661! Most of those mentioned had changed sides or given the impression of doing so. Was this an orgy of preference falsification on their parts or evidence that for many prominent individuals allegiance to anything beyond material interest was really quite shallow?

Edmund Waller was among the most bare-faced of the Vicars of Bray. He was an immensely rich man to whom the £10,000 fine imposed when he was exiled in 1644 was of no special consequence. In his view, heritable property was the key to all other rights. He was desperately afraid of the mob and apprehensive of the power of the church, the latter fear being his reason for turning down Aubrey's request to write a poem praising the free-thinking Thomas Hobbes. After 'Waller's plot', a revolt of 1643 supposedly promoting middle-of-the-road policies but devolving into intimations of armed rising, he sat in jail protesting his (current) loyalty and was alleged to have bribed the entire House of Commons one by one.

Waller was Cromwell's second cousin by marriage, which must have eased his return from exile in 1651. By then he had penned a 'Panegyrick to my lord Protector'. Lucy Hutchinson is thought to have been the author of a line-by-line refutation of this Panegyrick, so resistant were hard-core anti-monarchists to the notion of elevating Cromwell to near-kingship. The modal attitude of Parliamentarians was softer than hers and they proved less than vehemently opposed to kingship when it was embodied in the returning Charles II. As for Waller, he quickly squirmed around in 1660 to write a poem on 'his Majesties Happy Return.' Maybe preference falsification was not the term for this, but the falsity was transparent and recognised as such by his contemporaries. His all-purpose flattery nevertheless worked. His descendants were able to hold onto their own and we have his grandson to thank for the superb garden at Hall Place, Beaconsfield, the mansion that Edmund Waller had built.

Many men scrambled to make their peace with the Restoration regime. Even officers of the parliament sometimes re-emerged in acceptable guise, as did the 'formidable' Colonel John Birch, who served almost twenty further years in post-Restoration parliaments as a member for Weobley, Herefordshire, where a huge statue to him still stands in the parish church. More significant than the flexibility of the arts establishment, then, was the crossover of individuals who became or remained influential in political or policy circles. Former Cromwellians were actually among the clique of eight that ran the Clarendon administration from summer 1660 to autumn 1667. Seven of the eight have full entries in the *Dictionary of National Biography*, starting with Edward Hyde, Earl of Clarendon, another man with Wiltshire roots. One of the remainder, Lord Berkeley, was brother to the governor of Virginia. The member missing from the *DNB* is the elusive Martin Noel. In only one of the entries for the remaining seven, that of the sole other merchant in the clique, Thomas Povey, is Noel so much as mentioned. Among the remaining members, George Downing made sure to ingratiate himself with Charles II by going in for what has been called 'royalist over compensation' and paying his way, so to speak, by introducing Dutch financial practices to England.

Noel and Povey were useful to the pragmatic Charles despite having been deeply implicated in the Cromwellian regime. Noel was Spymaster Thurloe's brother-in-law and was principal banker to Cromwell's government. According to Povey, who should have known, he had been in 'extraordinary favour' with the Protector. Noel and Povey both helped to fit out the 'Western Design' fleet for the West Indies in 1654 and the next year Noel petitioned Cromwell for a warrant to supply 2,000 dozen shoes and 300 dozen boots to islands in the Caribbean. Sir Andrew Riccard was another merchant busy with the Western Design. He was not one of the charmed circle of eight 'interlocking directors' but merits an aside because he illustrates what might be thought the duplicity of the times because in Puritanical 1656 he had taken the risk of arranging a private episcopal blessing on his daughter's wedding.

West Indies' connections and expertise were what helped these men to skip across the Restoration divide and become as valuable to Charles II as they had been to Cromwell. Together with the true Royalists among the eight, the former Parliamentarians sat variously on the Privy Council, the Board of Trade and Plantations, the East India Company, and something that would have given Noel no qualms at all, the new African slave trade corporation. Because they were convinced mercantilists they devised the Navigation Acts of 1660 and 1663. To achieve their ends they were not above manipulating the length of sittings of the House of Commons. They came up with the Clarendon Code, which elevated the Anglican Church while suppressing its rivals. These were policy settings that persisted in essence for an abnormally long time. Later politicians debated but largely failed to overturn them. The Elite Settlement under Charles II thus embraced policies that had been developed under Cromwell. The policies had staying power; and the two otherwise very different scholars, Christopher Hill and William Dodd, therefore lit on the fifteen years or so that spanned the Restoration divide as going a long way towards shaping the long-term course of history. When the previous fifteen years during which so many Royalists had moved to Virginia and Maryland are added, it can be seen that the events of the middle decades of the seventeenth century made a virtually indelible mark on the economy of both sides of the Atlantic.

The Restoration of 1660 and Glorious Revolution of 1688 sealed the emergent history of eighteenth- and nineteenth century England which the policy settings established. 'The principles on which government has been conducted have not varied from the Revolution of 1688 to the present time', wrote John Wade in the 1820s. This denotes the longevity of seventeenth-century arrangements. The 1650s had already thrown up innumerable creative ideas, for example hypothetical constitutions, but one of their tangible and abiding legacies was certifying and preserving the system of landed estates. With this they solidified a settlement in England more unequal than the one achieved at Independence in the United States by a similar elite, who by then had the additional writings of Locke, Montesquieu and Rousseau for reference. It was not that the plantation owners in the American colonies had any affection for rednecks but rather that the backwoodsmen in their coonskin caps had the escape valve of the abundant land opening up in the United States soon after Independence. Poor Englishmen were more easily cabined, cribbed, and confined.

8

ECONOMIC SEQUEL

INITIAL REACTIONS AND revenge apart, the aftermath of the upsets and uncertainties of the Civil War and Interregnum periods was surprisingly promising. It must have seemed unexpectedly benign to contemporaries. Within a very few years the immediate vengefulness marking the return of Charles II was curbed. The sections of a primarily landed society that had been at war with itself returned to the plough and rather soon settled to business more or less as usual. What did the settlement achieve? Its own perpetuation for a start. Abandoning the dreams of extremists like the Levellers, the grip that landowners had always maintained on the countryside was intensified, not loosened, while during the following decades and centuries, agriculture became more productive. This is the paradox: a repressive estate system largely dedicated to status, pleasure and amenity co-existed with agricultural advance.

Land was central to the subsequent enriching of England for at least four reasons. First, its ownership provided the entree to local, regional and national politics. Secondly, came its obvious contribution of food. Thirdly, there was its less obvious but very significant and growing contribution of non-food products. Fourthly came its major role in shedding a high proportion of one of its own main inputs, labour, while succeeding in raising output. Part of the rural population was continually drifting into the towns and moving in stages towards London.

Under any regime, land remained crucial to the safe-keeping of capital and a continual source of income for the bulk of the wealthy classes. Trade and finance might be more profitable yet were disagreeably vulnerable to the shifting winds of commerce. Defoe was soon to say that trade is a spring but land is a pond, yet estates functioned as the equivalents of bank accounts in an era before trustworthy banks had emerged. Accordingly capital from other sectors of the economy was deposited in land and the rents that tenant farmers paid for use of the fields can be seen as the interest on it. Add in the attractions of social position and political access and estates exerted the pulling power they have retained through the centuries. For a considerable period agriculture remained the largest sector of the economy and its course, managed at the local level by the gentry, was ultimately steered by the enormous political power of the landed magnates. Some cavalier landlords spread new crops and intensive methods they had learned about in exile. When they met in London on parliamentary business or during the social season they were to be found discussing new ideas about husbandry. Within a generation they were bold enough to protect arable farming by encouraging the export of grain. That this could be done with little sign of excessive privation or famine among the mass of the population is testimony to agriculture's development.

Clearly there was more to improvement than the role of the leading landowners; the impetus was more widespread and labour productivity rose thanks to competition and effort among ordinary farmers. The pace was stately rather than swift, but intensification continued. Fresh, less personal, modes of transmitting information appeared. From at least the late eighteenth century, local newspapers took to printing reports of new methods. Further sources of information and emulation were eventually created in the form of agricultural societies offering prizes for technically superior products. Admittedly the societies were commonly founded and dominated by great landowners who had an interest in stimulating the productivity of their tenant farms. The downside was that agricultural shows fostered the 'prize marrow fallacy' by rewarding the technical perfection of animals and crops. This was not self-evidently efficient from the economic point of view: there were prizes for fat cattle but no public awards for maximum rates of return on agricultural investment.

Given the uncertainty that preceded 1660 and which was not quite a closed book thereafter, the successful development of agriculture may seem surprising. It should however be remembered that economic recovery had begun quickly after the execution of Charles I in 1649. Royalists too seem to have been active during the Interregnum because they needed to recoup what they had lost in fines for allegiance to the monarch and because, being now excluded from political life, they spent more time on their estates. The endorsement of the Cromwellian economy by Bishop Burnet of Salisbury is worth quoting again, 'We always reckon those eight years of usurpation a time of great peace and prosperity.' The underlying strength of the economy is evident. If one sets aside the more newsworthy political incidents, the history of the second half of the seventeenth century might be written as a series of 'bounce-backs' to a trend of productivity and prosperity that continued upwards. It is indicative that in 1671 Aubrey noted how the poorest people had glass in their windows, which they could not have afforded a generation earlier.

For more than two centuries after the Restoration the rural economy was ever more organised along estate system lines. This was orderly but nevertheless a deadweight cost to the economy, despite encouraging some new techniques and despite the fashion for farming set by George III. We must not be mesmerised by the conspicuous houses and parks of the landed elite or by their social and political prominence. These features attract attention but other modes of business organisation might have used resources in a more efficient and indisputably more equitable way. Advance did not occur because the arrangement of landownership was economically optimal or through hypothesised revolutions in property rights. What may the alternative have been? The answer is a society of small or medium-sized farms run by independent, literate owner-occupiers with access to information markets. Something along these lines was already emerging in north-west England before the Restoration, with pregnant consequences for the industrialisation that was to grow out of it. But in most districts farms were increasingly being engrossed by landowners, leading eventually to the grotesquely unbalanced profile of ownership recorded in the New Domesday of 1870.

Estates were consumption goods as much or more than they were productive firms. Their resources were often squandered. Landowners hired stewards to run them and liked the money from rents, although those with big extra-agricultural resources did not need to rely on income from tenanted farms. The accepted rate of return to estate land was under two per cent, which was less than might have been obtained in commercial or industrial enterprises. Capital was thus immobilised in properties that may seem to have been run purely as businesses but were primarily status symbols. Spending was diverted into building enormous houses and filling them with what the taste of the owner deemed to be great art and employing large numbers of people on fruitless activities like domestic service. The minimum possible was spent on housing the workers (indoors and out), and able people were allocated to a nugatory layer of bureaucracy employed in managing the land. The fact that mansions, parks and artworks are the objects of veneration by certain types of scholar and by the visitors who crowd into houses open to the public should not disguise the frivolity that took resources away from purposeful ends during the crucial centuries of England's growth. The modern tourist trade is an unintended consequence of self-interested expenditure on luxuries made at a time when many in the population were desperately poor.

Adopting the categories customarily used to evaluate the performance of economic systems may put order into the discussion of the landed economy. There are seven categories according to which performance is judged: full resource mobilization, resilience to shocks, static and dynamic allocative efficiency, static and dynamic technical efficiency, and income equality. These are dry terms but they are enlightening because the list of categories is comprehensive and can be replicated for different periods or compared among different countries. Strict measurement is not possible and assessing performance ultimately involves semi-subjective choices, yet taken together the criteria do offer a standard. Because agriculture accounted for such a massive share of the national economy at the Restoration and continued to be enormous two centuries later, the approach can be used to sketch the contribution of the sector (and the estate system) to the development of the whole economy.

With due allowance for intervening developments, suitable benchmark dates might be about 1680, once the Restoration settlement had time to bed down, and about 1880, on the brink of the great arable depression. Although agriculture's share in the economy contracted earlier and faster than anywhere else except the United Provinces of the Netherlands, about 36 per cent of the occupied population in England was still to be found in agriculture, forestry and fishing in 1801, 28 per cent at the start of reliable statistical data in 1841, and 17 per cent as late as the census of 1881. The shrinkage of the rural economy does make the task of assessing the sector's performance difficult. It means dealing with a moving target. But the shrinkage of the whole sector was presumably less than the figures for labour suggest, because there is no reason to think that capital or what the classical economists called capital-in-land (buildings, accommodation roads and so forth) was withdrawn as fast as workers left. The value of other factors may even have been on the increase.

As for the input of land, it too increased rather than shrank. This may sound paradoxical but really means that the use of the land was intensified. Cultivated and intensively grazed areas grew through enclosures of one form or another and where this led to changes of use it usually implied intensification. Nor should the method of 'rolling hedges' whereby thousands of small farmers increased the area of their farms at the expense of the adjacent 'waste' be forgotten. We lack figures or chronology for that advance, which is therefore overlooked by those seeking pre-digested statistics, but W. G. Hoskins' local study in Devon has shown its extent. It is also indicated in my work on the New Forest with the late Colin Tubbs.

These mentions of expansion in the farmed area and the greater use of land already under some less intensive form of agricultural occupation lead us to the first performance criterion, the full employment of available resources. The question of resource use is historically important because of the fashionable thesis that Europe, meaning north-western Europe and especially England, reached an 'organic ceiling' about 1800. Their economies were supposedly able to grow and industrialise only because raw materials could be seized in the American colonies and imported from there, and because coal was available to power steam engines.

The use of resources always depends on technology. This was improving over time and it became easier to grow crops on the poor soils that had hitherto been stigmatized as 'waste', grazed only by the commoners' unimpressive animals. Nevertheless, although the areal limits were being approached in the third quarter of the nineteenth century, not all such resources were fully exploited at any period. Too much land, often former farmland, had been converted into parkland, a process marked in the late eighteenth century by the establishment of parks in a vast ring around London leaving only traces of former cultivation in ploughing rig 'fossilised' under stretches of grass. By 1820 the map of England was thoroughly spattered with parks.

On working farms, maximum production was not always assured because to facilitate blood sports restrictive covenants were imposed, rotations altered and trees planted. There was nothing new about elite interest in blood sports, which was an ancient tradition among anyone with access to land – we saw that the Penruddock rebels cloaked their conspiracy with a week's fox-hunting, a pastime so popular among the gentry as not to attract notice even when Cromwell had banned horse-racing. What altered was the way in which this and other sports like coursing and shooting became crazes as the estate system waxed bigger during the eighteenth- and nineteenth centuries. Farming was shaped in ways that favoured these pastimes. The potential managerial talent, not merely of their employees but of the landed class itself – a Veblenesque leisure class - was devoted to these unproductive ends.

A parallel development was the privatisation of rivers for the sake of sport fishing, most famously described in Izaak Walton's *The Compleat Angler* (1653). Historians have consistently under-rated the economic impact of amenity considerations like these. It is worth dwelling on Walton for a moment, because his life so exemplifies the personal connections that the earlier chapters of this book repeatedly mentioned. He was a Royalist who was involved in the rescue of the 'Lesser George', the garter jewel lost by Charles II at the battle of Worcester in 1651, and he later became steward to the post-Restoration Bishop Morley, once incumbent of the Jones's parish of Minal. Walton first published his fishing book during the Interregnum and revised it over the next twenty-five years, another marker of elite continuity between periods. Meanwhile the withdrawal of inland fisheries into private hands deprived ordinary villagers of fish protein from their local waters. That Britain, which was described by Aneurin Bevan as an island of coal surrounded by fish, was in a position to replace river fish with sea-fish implies there was no net lack of resources.

Other considerations may seem to suggest on the contrary that biological resources were desperately scarce in England. For centuries it seemed so. Poor villagers scrabbled to find natural food and raw materials; they found uses for every plant in the countryside, purposes almost everywhere abandoned since the early twentieth century and now mostly forgotten. Historically, protein was scarce and was eaten in forms that would now be thought unpalatable, even noxious. Fuel for the fire was sought in every nook and cranny, something that became more and more difficult as woods were enclosed and commons cultivated.

No doubts can be entertained about scarcity in the old rural economy. Poor communications meant isolation and extreme localism, for instance it is reported that there were 100 local names for the early purple orchid, in this case not exactly a useful plant but the principle obtains. Rural people were confined to the vicinity of their homes by lack of transport and understandably scoured the lanes and hedgerows for anything they could eat or burn. This reflected poverty and limited mobility and the low opportunity costs of female or child labour, signalling distributional effects as much as gross shortages. The context is important because we may exaggerate the confidence with which even the prosperous looked on the supply of food. Before Victorian times people who were rich enough to have scant need to worry continued to be a little insecure, living as they did nearer to periods when harvests had failed and close to poor neighbours who still occasionally felt real want. They clung to their own forms of insurance and traditional ways. Great mansions were not ringed by the smooth lawns and luscious flower beds which are nowadays associated with houses open to the public. In the past orchards and kitchen gardens came up close.

One understandable point made in the literature about resource use is that food crops and woodland competed for space at the margin. Extending one meant reducing the other. The idea of a contest between the two uses derives from earlier historical studies of a 'timber famine' which supposedly meant that the production of charcoal to smelt iron had reached its limit. If more food were to be grown, it would have to be at the expense of wood for industry and domestic heating. This is formally correct, although by 1800 it was not really a problem. Trees are a crop and the supply of wood could be increased without necessarily taking in more land: for instance more charcoal could be obtained by shortening the coppice rotation, that is to say by cutting hazel rods at (say) every five years instead of seven.

Logically the organic economy did have limits but they were nowhere near reached when England started switching to coal as the source not merely of heat energy but for powering steam-driven machinery. More food was being grown without much discernible encroachment on forested land. The leading author on the transition from an organic to an inorganic economy, E. A. Wrigley, has himself calculated that agricultural output doubled between 1600 and 1831, despite the larger population at the latter date. Not much food was available to import, which was not the case with raw materials. On the few eighteenth-century occasions when the supply of iron seemed to be threatened, merchants quickly responded by importing more. England's was not an entirely closed economy. Moreover Wrigley has correctly observed that agricultural historians have concentrated too much on the production of foodstuffs when over the same long period the supply of non-food products from the land also expanded, and did so much faster than the rate of growth of population. We are observing a responsive agriculture that provided enough food and other goods (such as the large quantities of leather vital in a horse-drawn economy) while simultaneously permitting land to be withdrawn from productive uses to accommodate the aesthetic and sporting preferences of landowners.

A second and more immediate criterion of economic performance is resilience to shocks. Here we may start with Adam Smith's remark that during the 100 years from 1660 to 1760 there were seven wars, three rebellions, the Great Fire and the Plague yet, as he said, altogether they did not halt, 'the progress of England towards opulence.' Those one hundred years Smith called, 'the happiest and most fortunate period of them all.' Coming immediately after the destructive Civil wars and the uncertainties of the Interregnum, this was a remarkable achievement, the more so because it seems contrary to what might be deduced from the occurrence of upsets. In farming and commerce economic growth was already so deeply rooted that investment and activity bounced back after every interruption.

There were interruptions a-plenty. Besides the major shocks mentioned by Smith, the economy was continually beset by local incidents. English weather offered a series of unwelcome disturbances on all sides: late frosts, droughts and great heat, excessive rain, hail-storms, deep snow and so on and so forth. Hay-cocks floated down rivers, sheep suffered from liver rot, and harvests were battered by cold and wet. Because of the effect of volcanic dust in the atmosphere, 1816 was known as the 'year without a summer'. At the end of the period we are surveying the drenching rains of 1879 meant that 'the wheat came home sopping wet like manure.'

Many of the individual weather events cancelled out at the national level, with the damage confined to particular sites or regions, or to one type of agriculture. It has to be remembered how geologically and ecologically varied the English countryside is and how diverse its farming – the simplest illustration being that because grain is feed for animals, livestock farmers could gain from cereal prices low enough to hurt the pockets of arable producers. There were many such offsets varying from place to place and altering from month to month, let alone from year to year. They ensured that the distribution of harm done by the weather shifted like a shaken kaleidoscope. If many of the environmental 'insults' were thus highly specific, others did affect wide areas and sometimes raised the price of farm products steeply, even in an increasingly integrated market. Not only agriculture was affected. When manufacturing still depended on water power the mills were sometimes brought to a halt in dry years. The whole of a technologically weak production system was at risk.

Despite these set-backs, advances in farming methods made for more varied products and reduced losses as a whole. A succinct comment by Gilbert White illustrates this well. Referring to a spell of wet years from the early 1760s to 1773, he wrote that there had never 'been known a greater scarcity of all sorts of grain, considering the great improvements of modern husbandry. Such a run of wet seasons a century or two ago would, I am persuaded, have occasioned a famine.' The improvements arose from new rotations, new fodder crops and a raft of small, unsung changes in procedures. Parliamentary enclosure was involved, though less than is usually suggested; it is a topic to which attention is drawn because numerical data are available. Its significance has been exaggerated because some scholars citing these sources refer to the number of acts passed and awards made rather than to demonstrable advances in productivity.

Instead of noting legal measures a better first step might be counting the acres involved. This is seldom done, although the doyen of agricultural historians, W. E. Tate, long ago estimated the area affected in Nottinghamshire. His graphs show that less than half of the land there had been enclosed by the time Gilbert White wrote. Furthermore, figures supplied by Tate for the whole of England show that only four per cent of the total area ever subject to acts of parliament had been enclosed by 1760. Enclosure by agreement, which preceded parliamentary procedures and was cheaper to secure, did ensure that a large area was already affected, doubtless partly explaining White's observation that output had risen.

Much enclosure favoured a shift in ownership to the larger proprietors. Actual husbandry advances are seldom certified from farm records and may not have been rapid. Off the farm, better transportation did help, not only in getting produce to market but in sparking competition between farms and localities. Shifts in agricultural geography permitted specialisation. During the late seventeenth- and eighteenth centuries cultivation was able to spread onto the downs and wolds. Their light soils were easier to plough and incurred lower production costs. Concurrently farmers on the heavy soils of the clay vales reduced their cereal acreages and turned the land into pasture; this was a regional re-sorting that favoured efficiency. Food supplies became still more secure after the 1870s as a result of imports.

Towns and cities suffered their own types of shock, notably large-scale fires. The Great Fire of London was a colossus among conflagrations but it is less recognised that smaller towns were recurrently prone to serious fires. A survey (which did not claim to be complete) identified 500 major fires between 1500 and 1900. The lower bound for inclusion was ten houses destroyed by a single outbreak but some fires were much larger, consuming scores or hundreds of houses, as well as the barns, workshops and other buildings that tended to cluster close behind houses even in town centres. In addition there were innumerable one-, two- or three-house fires, besides village fires and others that destroyed warehouses containing goods or raw materials.

This scourge shows an interesting pattern in that the number of town fires peaked in the third quarter of the eighteenth century and fell off afterwards. The fall coincided with the spread of non-flammable building materials like brick and tile and with the rising prosperity that made them affordable. London was rebuilt after the Great Fire because in a trading city capital could be raised for the purpose. The same was widely true of small towns, not many of which waited long before rebuilding started. Admittedly workers' housing was sometimes rushed up in the same flammable materials as before, the clothing towns of East Devon being a particular sore spot that continued to be devastated into the nineteenth century. But what had been a major scourge in the early modern period was satisfactorily defeated, so that Adam Smith's point holds and the country's progress towards opulence was not held back. Opulence, or at any rate comfort, was evident in the market towns that ringed London, which participated in transporting rural produce to the capital and serviced their own surrounding farms.

'Resilience to shocks' sounds nicely scientific until we start to ask for definitions. Damage was inflicted by events of many types but whereas physical harm is relatively easy to observe in contemporary sources, and the immediate costs are sometimes computable, for example with harvest failures, floods or fires, losses in one activity could be offset by gains in another. Urban rebuilding could spur investment and economic activity more generally and employ materials that were proof against further disasters: it is an ill wind that blows no-one good. The web of relationships was intricate and we can advance little further than noting that, in many spheres and in the long term, the trend of loss fell over the period. Allowance must be made for the fact that more structures, goods, crops and livestock appeared after 1660, meaning that larger volumes of all these items were at risk. The fact that the number and scale of shocks fell nevertheless reinforces the conclusion that society was better able to ward them off. The concept of the 'fire gap' is useful here: if the population (as a proxy for urban capital at risk) and the number of urban fires are plotted together it is clear that the disasters not only decreased absolutely but were plunging relative to the population, especially from the third quarter of the eighteenth century. This is a crude but persuasive index demonstrating that resilience to shocks really was improving.

It is time to move on to the remaining markers of economic performance, the next four of which have the off-putting titles of static and dynamic allocative efficiency, and static and dynamic technical efficiency. The first of these, static allocative efficiency, requires making a judgement as to whether all economic resources are deployed to maximum effect at a given moment and cannot be moved to use elsewhere without loss. This ideal situation never obtains, there always having been occupations, industries and sectors that could have advantageously shed inputs to others. That much is true whatever date we choose. Distortions in policies and institutional forms were evident. They signalled rent-seeking whereby special interests with political power and influence rigged the law to give themselves disproportionate returns. The resultant protectionism always placed the equivalent of a tax on someone to the advantage of someone else. In the reign of William & Mary parliament became notoriously protectionist. Conspicuous consumption, which amounts to conspicuous waste, was also rife, as was the evil that William Cobbett labelled the Old Corruption.

Compared with what was feasible the economy was arthritic at all levels: for example guilds restricted entry to the trades in their town and in principle, as well as to some extent in practice, dictated the quantities of goods that might be produced, their quality, and the prices charged by those who were admitted. The precise consequences are hard to evaluate. Villages and small towns adumbrated rules and regulations galore, yet operated from day to day as associational communities (the sociologist Ferdinand Tonnies' term) in which people behaved according to conventions understood by all and where the motives for decisions were seldom written down. The workings of one such community in the nineteenth century are penetratingly described in Richard Jefferies, *Hodge and his Masters*. A writer of 1776 noted that England had good laws but they were 'shamefully neglected in their execution.' For all these reasons it cannot be held that resources were optimally allocated. They never are, but the situation was patently unsatisfactory in the seventeenth and eighteenth centuries. That the economy grew despite such handicaps may seem remarkable.

Determining either the state of play or the rate of change in the economy for two generations after the Restoration with any exactitude is scarcely possible. The available sources are thin but while a near-contemporary observer like Gilbert White knew change had taken place, historians show next-to-no interest in the central matter of husbandry practice. We can make only provisional assessments that lead us to think continuity tended to dominate or more precisely that there were more short-run political interruptions than serious breaks of trend. The sowing and harvesting of crops followed their old seasonal routines. Farm operators may have been perturbed by the events of high politics but were seldom brought to a standstill. Political sources emphasize disturbance but the reality was a high degree of temporising by the gentry class as it accommodated to every regime change in the second half of the seventeenth century. Given our distance in time, it is reasonable to view the agricultural economy as progressing steadily through even great upsets like the fall of James II and invasion by William III.

What, then, of dynamic allocative efficiency? Despite initial misallocations, were resources continually being moved to where they could be employed to best advantage? In other words were resources being reallocated to their points of best use? Obstruction by special interests says not. Yet some loosening of restrictions can be detected. Guild, borough and parish regulations were flouted, as can be deduced from the endless presentments for failing to observe them. Elites accepted more market competition in place of rent-seeking. This is the most enigmatic of all economic changes and began well back in early modern times. In 1599 the courts struck down the right of guilds to confiscate the goods of someone they deemed to be working in a town illegally. Within a very few years the courts removed the power of prohibiting 'strangers' from practising their trade without acquiring, that is to say paying for, 'freedom of the borough' and accepting its guild restrictions.

Whereas the judges cannot be passed off as economic liberals, the common law did contain tendencies of the sort, descending from the publication in 1630 by John Haviland, Miles Flesher and Robert Young (themselves not free from playing fast and loose with the law) of Sir Edward Coke's *Institutes of the Lawes of England*. At the very end of the seventeenth century the judiciary obtained its independence from the crown and from parliament, and could free the market if it so wished. It did not automatically do so but built up case law that took on a life of its own, something different from either the ad hoc selling of favours by early Stuart kings or the protectionism espoused by parliaments.

The experience of re-allocative efficiency was decidedly mixed. Not everything was continually in process of moving to where it might earn the highest marginal return. Judged by an absolute standard, England fell short. Opportunities were not always seized despite the potential gain. Best practice did not spread automatically. Ancient institutions like courts leet or soke mills persisted to the mid-nineteenth century and later. Small farms were commonly held on copyhold, tenancy being guaranteed until the death of the last of three lives. Who the tenants were was not always easy to trace and descriptions of landed property could be vague and therefore contentious. Expensive interpretation by lawyers was needed. Yet sluggishness, friction and cost notwithstanding, the system proved more flexible than it might have done. In infinite little ways the economy was shuffling out of the straitjacket of custom.

How speedy a resource adjustment was to be expected is not clear, but judged by gross results rather than the spotty evidence of the array of imperfections, blockages and resistances to change, the late preindustrial and early industrial economy presents a story of success. It was less restricted by rules and impediments than most of continental Europe and the rise and fall of individual towns demonstrate the presence of considerable competition. This can be illustrated from the record of labour as a factor of production. Geographical mobility was marked, a conclusion that is not invalidated by the many cases when individuals were callously returned to their original places of settlement, which were held responsible if they fell sick. The mobility of labour and enterprise is attested by the steady shifts of population, notably movement into London (and out again to the suburbs to escape guild regulation). Industries decayed in the south of England but rose in the Midlands and North. Resources did therefore move around, however slow the movement may now appear. A crude indicator is that in 1650 eight out of the ten largest provincial cities were to be found in the south of the country, whereas by 1860 eight out of the ten largest were located in the north.

Moving on to static technical efficiency the question is whether the most productive known methods were everywhere in use. Again, that was clearly not true at any date. Considering only agriculture in the years immediately after the Restoration, some landowners who returned from exile were quick to introduce crops, especially fodder crops, which they had seen in the Low Countries. The period also saw a flowering of antiquarian writing which, while ostensibly backward-looking, encouraged thought about practical matters concerning resources, innovations, inheritance and land law. The great writers John Aubrey, William Dugdale, Robert Plot and their fellows were men of their times and rejected the taunt of their more present-minded contemporaries that they were mere dry-as-dust antiquaries. By modern standards they were like polymaths in their range of interests. Aubrey wrote in *Miscellanies Upon Various Subjects*, that 'inclosures are for the private, not for the public good' and that they were responsible for creating many poor people. Dugdale was well rewarded for using his antiquarian knowledge to bolster the insecure legal position of the Company of Adventurers in draining the Great Levels. Plot paid close attention to the geological resources of Oxfordshire as well as to novelties introduced by some of its inhabitants.

Efforts were made quickly after 1660 to generalise the adoption of novelties, as the activities of the newly-founded Royal Society show and as do fresh books about methods of farming. 'Since his Majesty's most happy Restoration,' wrote John Houghton in one of the *Agricultural Newsletters* he brought out soon after that event, 'the whole land hath been fermented and stirred up by the profitable hints it hath received from the Royal Society, by which means parks have been disparked, commons inclosed, woods turned into arable and pasture land improved by clover, sainfoin, turnips, coleseed, parsley and many other good husbandries, so that the food of cattle is increased as fast if not faster than the consumption.' This is not to say that agriculture had been inert under the Commonwealth, just that as far as we can tell the Restoration further energised it.

Different vintages of technology in use at the same moment were also visible in the next-largest group of industries, textiles. Best practice had a long way to go before it was fully adopted in societies with restricted sources of information, which leads us to the next category, dynamic technical efficiency. Were the best available methods being introduced at the optimal rate? 'Best' in this sense means so as to maximise the rate of return. We know from the lagged rates of adoption that technical problems were not always easy to overcome and are too readily smoothed away by historians writing *de haut en bas*. Information markets were seriously imperfect and enterprise was not as bold as it might have been, the sluggish replacement of charcoal in the manufacture of iron being a case in point. In many industries, resistance to innovation on the part of the workforce is also evident. Nevertheless reports of slow adoption may mask the true pace of change. Too often accounts start with the inception of statistics about some novelty or other, like the turnpike, and decry or ignore the small, slow, but proportionately as significant improvements already taking place.

Some agriculturists were notably experimental. Jethro Tull (kept in business because, as we have seen, Bulstrode Whitelocke stood surety for him) published *Horse-hoeing Husbandry* in 1731. Large landowners were the people most likely to read such books or at least hear about these things. Farmers who did not come into direct contact with formal points of innovation continued cultivating the open fields according to older fashions. They lacked capital as well as information, and were not infrequently locked into communal routines of husbandry that made it hard to step out ahead of their fellows. Like peasant farmers in less developed countries today, they did not have enough resources to feel safe trying something new which, while it might increase productivity, might also fail disastrously. Houghton's enthusiasm applied most to landowners but the novelties they embraced took time to spread downwards.

In industry changes were definitely occurring well before the classic industrial revolution period. Great gains were to be had even before mechanisation. Adam Smith pointed out that a watch costing £20 in the mid-seventeenth century was already 95 per cent cheaper and better made by 1776, something confirmed by modern research. The notion that fruitful techniques in every industry would be instantly taken up is however fanciful and even if we could measure adoption rates we would not know what pace it is reasonable to expect. Even so, new methods of production transformed many industries during the eighteenth and first half of the nineteenth centuries in a manner that may reasonably be called revolutionary compared with former times or most other countries. At a minimum this broadly implies dynamic technical efficiency, the very definition of an industrial revolution.

We now come to the last and most contentious criterion, equality of income. Within almost obvious but rather remote limits, the ideal degree of equality is a matter of judgement. On the one hand complete inequality would abolish the market yet on the other complete equality might remove all incentives. Given the extent of poverty coinciding with vaunting wealth, it may seem surprising that the post-Restoration and industrial revolution periods saw an approach – a distant one – towards the equality end of the spectrum. But the rise of new fortunes and the enlargement of the professional and managerial classes ate away at the medieval and early modern situation when the Crown and its rent-seeking entourage, together with a small number of great landowners and merchants, commanded the vast bulk of wealth. Industrialists and more unexpectedly successful retailers now joined the ranks of the super-rich. Numerous lesser entrepreneurs made modest fortunes, which might be called the rise of the bourgeoisie but was actually its enlargement. None of this softened the asperities of working class poverty; it is only a statistical observation and as has been said, statistics are frozen tears. Nevertheless, limited though it was, the direction of change lay towards some sharing of national wealth as well as the swelling of its volume. The conclusion is that the two post-Restoration centuries were more productive and prosperous than any earlier period, though this was more apparent in the towns than the countryside.

Assigning weights to the criteria put forward as a means of evaluating economic performance is ultimately out of the question. A mass of data survives about the changes that followed 1660 and endless suggestions have been made about their causes but no clear summary is forthcoming. National income accounts do not exist, apart from the heroic but unsubstantiated effort by Gregory King, which in any event refers to a single early period. An acceptable approach might be the indirect one of creating a long run index of physical changes, as is done for modern China, decide if it tracks the numerical data available for modern times, and then project it back. It is a vast task and there may not be enough components to construct a plausible index for earlier centuries. Data on food consumption and on demography as revealed in parish registers are full of gaps.

Recent work attempts to cut the Gordian Knot by using data from 921 skeletons from central and southern England to calculate the trend in average height, plausibly supposing this to be a proxy for health that is uncontaminated, as it were, by the deficiencies of other sources. The result is unexpected in that it is at odds with the rise of wages. GDP per capita rose during the seventeenth and eighteenth centuries whereas after 1650 height and life expectancy fell. The purported interpretation is that 'during the Industrial Revolution' the demands placed on workers rose, meaning more working days and worse working conditions, while incomes became less equal. But 'Industrial Revolution' can hardly be blamed for a trend starting as early as 1650 and it seems strained to point the finger at a preceding Industrious Revolution for being large enough to force down average height. Rising incomes and the greater output of the agricultural sector might have been expected to improve rather than worsen early nutrition. How far the wage-height divergence was a real phenomenon, as opposed to being an artefact of the sources, remains to be seen. The authors of the study admit, too, that an increasing percentage of their data comes from lower social and economic groups and from unhealthy London, which may create a more dismal picture than is warranted. Yet some measure of paradox may remain and as the authors declare, the feature of long-run English history most needing explanation is the period of low height from 1650-1800.

Fashions in interpretation continue to evolve. Reliance on the magic bullets of individual genius and new technology, which earlier economic historians emphasized and on which popularisers insist, has been replaced by an insistence that at the heart of the growth lay something in the realm of ideas or even culture, adding up to better human capital. It has however been suggested that studying the channels along which information flowed may be even more fruitful than concentrating on pure ideas or the people who conceived them, because ideas are easier to dream up than action is to take. Channels of information were vital. Fortunately postal services improved. Intellectuals of all types corresponded actively with one another in England and as far afield as the American colonies; at home they relied increasingly on institutionalised means of communication such as the Royal Society and the agricultural, scientific and local philosophical societies established during the two centuries after 1660.

Institutions have become prominent among explanations of economic growth. This is strongly expressed in the mantra claiming that property rights suddenly became secure in law after 1688 but this claim is rather unhistorical. Clearly there is a role for institutions in the complex of explanations but in some ways they should take a back seat. Perhaps they should sit a long way back because some of them were facing the wrong way (so to speak), meaning social, political and economic innovations that hampered growth or at least contributed little to it through rent-seeking. There is always an incentive to obtain a larger slice of the common cake rather than helping to bake a bigger one. For all this, despite the distortions of ownership, the agricultural sector did succeed in producing ever more food and industrial raw materials. Rent-seeking and the institutions that conduced to it were impediments and the market was left to counteract the drag they represented. In that it had some success although the distribution of the gains remained highly unequal. The economic system which was confirmed in the 1650s and 1660s perpetuated the inequality, as Christopher Hill and William Dodd understood. It confined much of the return to owning landed estates in England to a privileged margin of the population.

SOURCES
AND FURTHER READING

Prologue

On the value of regional studies, Alan Everitt, *The Local Community and the Great Rebellion* (London: The Historical Association, 1969) and Eric L. Jones, *Locating the Industrial Revolution: Inducement and Response* (Singapore: World Scientific, 2010). On the value of family histories, Anthony Wagner, *Pedigree and Progress: Essays in the genealogical interpretation of history* (London: Phillimore, 1975) should on no account be ignored. For an opposite interpretation to mine of the role of institutions, Douglas W. Allen, *The Institutional Revolution* (Chicago: University of Chicago Press, 2011). On the longevity of policy changes in the 1650s and 1660s taken together, William E. Dodd, 'The Emerge [sic] of the First Social Order in the United States', *American Historical Review* 40/2 (1935), pp.217-231, and Christopher Hill, *God's Englishman: Oliver Cromwell and the English Revolution* (London: Pelican, 1972), and for the inception of political stability, J. H. Plumb, *The growth of political stability in England, 1675-1725* (London: Palgrave Macmillan, [1967] 1977.

1: *Small Earthquake in Wiltshire*

Despite its absence from many national histories, the Penruddock Rising proves to have attracted a good number of accounts. Sources on the actual happening often overlap, as they do on many topics dealt with in later chapters. I have not attempted to present the whole kaleidoscope of references and do not specifically cite passing mentions in general histories, village histories that refer either to events in the period or the individuals concerned, or the valuable biographies in the *Dictionary of National Biography* and *History of Parliament*. Moreover I have not felt it helpful to list every long-vanished publishing house. Village histories seldom produce a high yield although parish sources and pamphlet church histories, when pieced together, can create pictures not readily available elsewhere. The parish website for Thurgarton, Nottinghamshire (mentioned in the text) is especially noteworthy as well as unexpectedly relevant. I also cite a few authorities from quite different fields who introduce interesting concepts or provide sidelights on the issues of the period. This is not taken very far but in my view local historians should not isolate themselves as much as they do from wider intellectual currents.

For the Rising itself, see S. T. Bindoff, 'Parliamentary History 1529-1688', *Victoria County History of Wiltshire* Vol. 5 (London: O.U.P n.d.); Sir Richard Colt Hoare, *The History of Modern Wiltshire: Salisbury* (London: John Bowyer Nichols & Son, 1843); Oliver Lawson Dick, *Aubrey's Brief Lives* (Harmondsworth, Middlesex: Penguin Books, 1962); Sir G. G. Duckett, 'The Royalist Rising in 1655 (from the Original Thurloe State Papers in the Bodleian Library)', *Wiltshire Archaeological Society Magazine* XIX (1881), pp.103-108; W. Macray Dunn, *Calendar of the Clarendon State Papers III (1655-1657)* (Oxford: Clarendon Press, 1876); Antonia Fraser, *Cromwell: Our Chief of Men* (London: Phoenix [1973], 2002); W. W. Ravenhill, 'Records of the Rising in the West A.D. 1655', *Wiltshire Archaeological Magazine* 13 No.28, pp.119-188; and A. H. Woolrych, *Penruddock's Rising 1655* (London: The Historical Association, 1973).

On counties adjacent to Wiltshire, see Andrew M. Coleby, *Central Government and the Localities: Hampshire 1649-1689* (Cambridge: Cambridge University Press, 1987); David Eddershaw, *The Civil War in Oxfordshire* (Stroud: Sutton, 1995); Kate Tiller and Giles Darkes (eds.), *An Historical Atlas of Oxfordshire* (Finstock: Oxford Record Society, 2010); A. R. Warmington, *Civil War, Interregnum and Restoration in Gloucestershire, 1640-1672* (Woodbridge: Royal Historical Society and Boydell Press, 1997); Tim Goodwin, *Dorset in the Civil War 1625-1665* (Tiverton: Dorset Books, 1996), and on the Clubmen especially Chris Bellers <Fonthill Magna.net/2013/10/the-dorset-clubmen>

On the nature of conspiracies, Timur Kuran, *Private Truths, Public Lies: The Social Consequences of Preference Falsification* (Cambridge, Mass.: Harvard University Press, 1995); David Underdown, *Royalist Conspiracy in England, 1649-1660* (New Haven: Yale University Press,

1960); Julian Whitehead, *Cavalier and Roundhead Spies: Intelligence in the Civil War and Commonwealth* (Barnsley: Pen and Sword Books, 2009); and I learned much from Mark Harrison, 'Counter-Intelligence in a Command Economy', Buckingham University Economics Seminar, 2015.

2: Defeat and Capture

Thomas Birch (ed.), *A Collection of the State Papers of John Thurloe, December 1654-September 1655, III* (1742); Rapin de Thoyras, *The History of England* Volume II (1760); Alice Dryden (ed.), *Memorials of Old Wiltshire* (London: Benrose & Sons, 1906); Andrew Hopper, *Turncoats and Renegades: Changing Sides during the English Civil Wars* (Oxford University Press, 2012); E. H. Lane Poole, *Damerham and Martin: A Study in Local History* (Tisbury: Compton Russell, 1976); J. T. Cliffe (ed.), 'The Cromwellian Decimation Tax of 1655: The Assessment Lists', *Camden Miscellany* 5th ser. 7 (1996); R. C. Richardson, *Town and Countryside in the English Revolution* (Manchester University Press, 1992); J.W. Bund Willis-Bund, *Diary of Henry Townshend* (Worcestershire Historical Society, 1920); and Willis Bund Willis-Bund, *A Selection of Cases Trials. Trials for Treason, Volume 1* (London: Forgotten Books [1879] 2013).
On transportation to Barbadoes: Greville Chester, *Transatlantic Sketches* (London: Smith, Elder, 1869); Peter Linebaugh, *The Many-Headed Hydra: Sailors, Slaves, Commoners and the Hidden History of the Revolutionary Atlantic* (Boston: Beacon Press, 2000); and Peter Rushton and Gwenda Morgan, *Banishment in the Early Atlantic World: Convicts, Rebels and Slaves* (London: Bloomsbury Academic, 2013).

3: Memorials of the Seventeenth Century

This chapter mainly derives from visits to churches and other historical sites in Southern England and beyond, together with numerous church and parish history pamphlets. But for Henry Marten see also Nicholas Davenport, *The Honour of St. Valery* (London: Scolar Press, 1978) and Byron Rogers, *The Bank Manager and the Holy Grail* (London: Aurum Press, 2003).

4: The Third Man

The histories of Oliver Cromwell's Wiltshire relatives and in particular Francis Jones (the third principal in the Rising), Francis's forebears at Minal (Mildenhall), his kinfolk the Cranes, his mother's family the Ryves of Dorset, and of Nathaniel Fiennes, who acquired Francis's Newton Tony estate, are tangled and sometimes highly obscure. The more fugitive sources are not reported here in order to avoid overwhelming the reader with references.

Francis Jones, his forebears and associates:
Anon., Indenture between David Waterhouse and James Bourchier *et al.* re Newton Tony manor, *Wiltshire Archaeological Magazine* XXVI (1909-1910); Anon., *Register of Admissions to the Honorable Society of the Middle Temple* Volume 1: Fifteenth Century to 1781 (London, 1949); John Aubrey, *The Natural History of Wiltshire* (London: J. B. Nichols, 1847); Joseph Bettey (ed.), *Wiltshire Farming in the Seventeenth Century* (Trowbridge: Wiltshire Record Society, 2005); R. Boucher, 'Oliver Cromwell's Wiltshire relatives', *Wiltshire Notes & Queries* VII (1911-1913), pp.25-32; Documents relating to the Goddard Family of North Wiltshire (Swindon Public Libraries, 1960 and second series, 1969); E. C. Elwell, Account of the Manor of Stratton St. Margaret, Typescript 1928 (Wiltshire Local Studies Library); George S. Fry and Edward Alex Fry (eds.), *Abstracts of Wiltshire Inquisitiones Post Mortem* (London: Wiltshire Archaeological Society, 1901); S. R. Gardiner, *History of the Commonwealth and Protectorate III 1654-1656* (London: Longman, Green, & Co., 1901); Lucy Hutchinson, *Memoirs of the Life of Colonel Hutchinson* (London: H. G. Bohn, 1863); John Edward Jackson, *Wiltshire: The Topographical Collection of John Aubrey, F.R.S., A.D.1659-70* (Devizes: Wiltshire Archaeological Society, 1862); E. G. H. Kempson, Manuscript collection, Wiltshire Archaeological Society Library, Devizes; Richard H. Luce, *The History of the Abbey and Town of Malmesbury* (Malmesbury: The Friends of Malmesbury Abbey, 1979); Mark Noble, *Memoirs of the protectorate-house of Cromwell, Volume 1* (Birmingham: 1787); Anthony Powell, *John Aubrey and his Friends* (London: The Hogarth Press, revised edition 1983); Richard Ollard, *The Escape of Charles II after the Battle of Worcester* (New York: Charles Scribner's Sons, 1966); Marigold M. Routh, *Amport: The Story of a Hampshire Parish* (Privately printed, 1986);

Peter Sherlock (ed.), *Sir Thomas Phillipps: Monumental Inscriptions of Wiltshire 1822* (Trowbridge: Wiltshire Record Society, 2000); Thomas Wagstaff, *A Vindication of K. Charles the Martyr* (London: R. Wilkin, third edition 1711); Mark Wareham, 'The Dodingtons of Mere – a "ruined" family', *www.southwilts.com/site/My-family-history.../dodingtoncw.pdf*; James Waylen, *A History Military and Municipal of the town of Marlborough* (London: John Russell Smith, 1854).

Ryves family:
Payne Fisher, *The tombes, monuments, and sepulchral inscriptions, lately visible in St. Paul's Cathedral* (London: Privately printed, 1684); W. Patrick Reaves, *The Ryves-Rives-Reaves Families of Europe and America* (Privately printed, 1999).

Nathaniel Fiennes:
Anon., 'Inventory of Goods of Nathaniel Fiennes, died 1669', *Cake and Cockhorse* 9/2 (1983), pp.138-148; Nicholas Allen, *Broughton Castle and the Fiennes family* (Adderbury: Wykeham Press, 2010); Alfred Beesley, *History of Banbury* (London: Nichols and Son, 1841); D. E. M. Fiennes, 'The Will of Nathaniel Fiennes (died 1669)', *Cake and Cockhorse* 9/5 (1984), pp.143-147.

5: Shocks, Retribution, Fusion

Anon, *Eastbury: A Berkshire Village* (Lambourne Valley Press, 2003); G. E. Aylmer and J. S. Morrill (eds.), *J. P. Cooper: Land, Men and Beliefs: Studies in Early-Modern History* (London: The Hambledon Press, 1983); Gilbert Farthing, *The Country-City "Alliance" of Cromwellian England 1658-1660* (M.A. thesis, University of British Columbia, 1962); D. H. Fischer, *Albion's Seed* (Oxford University Press, 1989); Charles Fitzroy, *Return of the King: The Restoration of Charles II* (Stroud: Sutton Publishing, 2007); K. H. D. Haley, *Charles II* (London: The Historical Association, 1966); Lawrence E. Hill, 'The Confederate Exodus to Brazil', *Southwestern Historical Quarterly* (October 1935 and January-April, 1936); Stephen Porter, *Destruction in the English Civil Wars* (Stroud: Sutton, 1997) – this last volume is the most comprehensive study of the wartime physical damage and its legacy.

6: Restoration and Sublimation

Archaeologia: a Miscellany of Tracts relating to Antiquity III (London, 1787); G. E. Aylmer (ed.), *The Interregnum: The Quest for Settlement 1646-1660* (London: Macmillan, 1974 edition); Emily Cockayne, *Cheek by Jowl: A History of Neighbours* (London: Vintage Books, 2013); Norman Hidden, *Aspects of the Early History of Hungerford* (Hungerford Historical Association, 2009); Michael Hunter, 'New Light on "The Drummer of Tedworth": Conflicting Narratives of Witchcraft in Restoration England', *Historical Research* 78 ([2001] 2005), pp.311-353; Molly McClain, *Beaufort: The Duke and his Duchess 1657-1715* (New Haven: Yale University Press, 2001); Roger Scruton, *Our Church: A Personal History of the Church of England* (London: Atlantic Books, 2012); A. R. Stedman, *Marlborough and the Upper Kennet Country* (Marlborough: Privately printed, 1960); A. W. Ward *et al.* (eds.), *The Cambridge Modern History, IV, The Thirty Years War* (Cambridge University Press [1906] 1969); David C. Whitehead, *Henley-on-Thames: A History* (Chichester: Phillimore, 2007).

7: Animal Farm and Elite Settlement

Jerry Brotton, *The sale of the late King's Goods: Charles I and His Art Collection* (London: Pan Macmillan, 2007); Mrs Chafin: Letter to Thomas Chafin from his wife [daughter of John Penruddock], 1688 *Gentleman's Magazine* 87/2 (1817); Antonia Fraser, *King Charles II* (London: Book Club Associates, 1979); Basil Duke Henning, *The House of Commons, 1660-1690* (London: Secker & Warburg, 1983); [Robert Jenner], Ordinance to divide Meysey Hampton from Marston Meysey, House of Lords *Journal* Volume 10 (1648), pp.219-222; Don Jordan and Michael Walsh, *The King's Revenge: Charles II and the Greatest Manhunt in British History* (London: Abacus, 2013); Dacher Keltner, *The Power Paradox: How we gain and lose influence* (London: Allen Lane, 2016); John Kenyon, *The Civil Wars of England* (London: Weidenfeld & Nicolson, 1988); John Kenyon, *The History Men* (London: Weidenfeld & Nicolson, second edition 1993); Alexander Larman, *Blazing Star: The Life and Times of John Wilmot, Earl of Rochester* (London: Head of Zeus, 2015 edition); Tim Mowl and Brian Earnshaw, *Architecture without Kings: The Rise of Puritan Classicism* (Manchester: Manchester University Press, 1995);

E. Roberts and M. Gale, 'Henry Mildmay's New Farms, 1656-1704', *Proceedings* of the Hampshire Field Club and Archaeological Society 50 (1995), pp.169-192; Joan Thirsk, 'The Restoration Land Settlement' in Joan Thirsk, *The Rural Economy of England: Collected Essays* (London: The Hambledon Press, 1984); Jenny Uglow, *A Gambling Man: Charles II and the Restoration 1660-1670* (London: Faber and Faber, 2009); John Wade, *The Black book, or, Corruption unmasked* (new edition, 1829).

8: Economic Sequel

Here we move even more decisively to national issues. The chapter surveys the long-run development of the economy after the Restoration and, although documenting this fully is impossible, indicative references are to be found in my other works, listed below. They include regional material and contain detailed end-notes: E. L. Jones, 'The European Background' in Stanley L. Engerman and Robert E. Gallman (eds.), *The Cambridge Economic History of the United States, Volume I: The Colonial Era* (Cambridge: Cambridge University Press, 1996), where the economic systems approach used in the present book is introduced, and Eric Jones, 'The Context of English Industrialization', in Avner Greif *et al.*, *Institutions, Innovation and Industrialization* (Princeton N.J.: Princeton University Press, 2015). See also Gregori Galofre-Vila *et al.*, 'Height Across the Last 2000 Years in England', Oxford Economics *Discussion Paper* 151 (January 2017). Eric L. Jones, 'Economics without History: objections to the rights hypothesis', *Continuity & Change* 28/3 (2013), pp.323-346, dissents from the fashionable opinion that 1688 represented the fundamental turning-point, on which compare Steven C. A. Pincus and James A. Robinson, 'What Really Happened During the Glorious Revolution?', NBER *Working Paper* 17206 (2011). Christopher W. Brooks, *Lawyers, Litigation and English Society since 1450* (London: The Hambledon Press, 1998) is informative.

INDEX

English place names

BERKS Anvills 88; Ashbury [now Oxon] 30; Ashdown House [now Oxon] 68, 88; Faringdon [now Oxon] 77, 87; Hampstead Marshall 68; Hungerford 5, 26, 30, 76, 88; Longworth [now Oxon] 29; Newbury 61; Pusey [now Oxon] 76; Shrivenham [now Oxon] 2, 29, 30, 71, 80; Speenhamland 19

BUCKS Hall Barn, Beaconsfield 88

CAMBS Haslingfield 27, 90; Wisbech Castle 87-88

CORNWALL Flushing 8, 26

DEVON East Devon 103; Exeter 10, 11, 14, 15, 17, 18, 20; South Molton 11, 13, 45

DORSET Beaminster 19, 51, 52, 69; Blandford 5, 10, 42, 43; Dorchester 10; Forde Abbey 88; Hambledon Hill 5; Ransdon, Iwerne Courteney 42, 43; Upwood 26, 41, 42; Wimborne St Giles 29

GLOS Gloucestershire vii, 2, 10, 60, 69, 70; Badminton 69; Coln St Denis 28; Coln St Aldwyn 73; Fairford 77; Gloucester 27, 34; Highnam Court 69; Horton 80; Meysey Hampton 84; Quenington 29, 64; Sherborne 80, 84; Tetbury 80; Williamstrip 64

HANTS Hampshire 10, 74; Amport 55; Binstead 20; Hungerford (New Forest) 5, 26; Moyles Court, Ellingham 64, 88; Tytherley 26, 45, 64, 75; Whitchurch 61, 62; Winchester 8, 40, 64, 68, 76

HEREFS Herefordshire 11, 20, 30, 48, 69, 79, 80, 87, 91; Richard's Castle 80; Ross-on-Wye 48, 87; Stretton Grandison 30, 69; Weobley 91

HUNTS Hinchinbroke 42, 49; Thorpe Hall 88

LANCS Lancashire 60

LEICS Leicestershire vi, vii

LONDON vi, 1, 8, 13, 14, 16, 20, 27, 32, 49, 52, 56, 57, 61, 68, 78, 82, 94, 95, 98, 103, 106, 110

NORTHANTS Northamptonshire vi, vii, 81

NOTTS Nottinghamshire 46, 56, 57, 102; Nottingham 46, 56, 58, 89; Thurgarton 46, 56, 57

OXON Oxfordshire 2, 13, 30, 52, 54, 69, 77, 107; Black Bourton 30; Bletchingdon 54; Glympton 52;

General Index